TESTIMONY OF TRIUMPH

By John M. Drescher

Follow Me
Now Is the Time to Love
Prayers for All Seasons
Spirit Fruit
Testimony of Triumph
Way of the Cross and the Resurrection

TESTIMONY OF TRIUMPH

THE MEANING OF CHRIST'S WORDS FROM THE CROSS

JOHN M. DRESCHER

ZONDERVAN PUBLISHING HOUSE
OF THE ZONDERVAN CORPORATION
GRAND RAPIDS, MICHIGAN 49506

Dedicated to Ellrose Zook, humble servant of Christ and the church: a long-time personal friend, one who always brought encouragement to me while I served as an editor under his able leadership, and one who, in addition to being a real friend, stands as an example of Christlike service and sacrifice.

TESTIMONY OF TRIUMPH

Grand Rapids, Michigan

Scripture quotations are from the King James Version of the Bible, unless otherwise noted.

Library of Congress Cataloging in Publication Data

Drescher, John M
Testimony of triumph.
1. Jesus Christ—Seven last words—Meditations.
I. Title.
BT456.D67 232.9'635 79-25962
ISBN 0-310-23920-6

Printed in the United States of America

Contents

The words of Christ
From the cross
And their application
Today—

Preface

More than fifteen hundred years ago, on Good Friday, Bishop Ambrose ascended his pulpit in the Cathedral of Milan and addressed his congregation. He said, "I find it impossible to speak to you today. The events of Good Friday are too great for human words. Why should I speak while my Savior is silent and dies?"

This sense of awe, wonder, and inability to comprehend all the meaning of the cross is the first thing which confronts us when we think of Good Friday. What can we say? Does not the cross say enough? Is not the ground so holy that one should not tread upon it? Are not the words which flow from the dying Savior too sacred even to speak about?

In another sense, when we begin to understand the meaning of Christ's words from the cross, we cannot be quiet. We must speak. We cannot forget. The life and heart of Christ is opened to us in a wondrous way. We hear and we begin to understand His unspeakable love.

> Seven times He spoke, seven words of love,
> And all three hours, His silence cried
> For mercy on the souls of men:
> Jesus, our Lord, was crucified.
>
> —Author Unknown

Fridtof Nansen, the great polar explorer, sounding the depth of the arctic seas, one day came to a spot where all his lines would not touch the bottom. When the last foot of line was let out, they tied on every piece of rope and cord on deck. Sheets were ripped up and strips of cloth tied to the line. Still the plummet did not rest on the bottom. That day Nansen wrote in the ship's log the total depth fathomed and added, "Deeper yet." His experience calls to mind the words concerning the cross—

> Through all the depth of sin and loss
> Drops the plummet of the cross;
> Never yet abyss was found
> Deeper than the cross can sound!

Down through the years many books have been written to help us plumb the depth of sin, to help us understand the significance of Calvary. Today there is a dearth of writings about the cross and particularly about the seven times that Jesus spoke from the cross. These utterances of Christ are known as the "seven last words of Jesus" or "the seven words of the cross." Yet, in a most striking way, the words of Jesus from the cross tell us the essential meaning of Christ's coming and death.

This book on Christ's words from the cross is shared with the deep desire that readers may see, not only the centrality of the cross for salvation, but also the centrality of the cross in enabling us to live the Christ life.

These messages were written to help the reader identify with the cross for salvation. But they do not stop there. They also insist on an identification with the cross to the point that we die to the old life and walk in newness of life.

"If we approach the cross for *examination,*" said Dr. G. Campbell Morgan, "it will evade us. If we approach it for *contemplation,* it will bewilder us. The only way to approach and understand the cross is by *identification.*"

Christianity Today editorialized: "A searching test of any minister's preaching is for him to ask about his every sermon, 'Have I in some way preached Christ crucified in this message?' Not that every sermon must follow an evangelistic stereotype nor that it must refer at length to the cross; preaching must be as varied as human life and its needs. But always, whether the sermon deals with social justice, moral problems, life situations, history, or prophecy, Christ crucified must be in it. He must be there if for no other reason than that no minister can know whether his is the last voice to reach some listener whose heart is open to receive new life in Christ. Preaching devoid of the Good Friday truth may be eloquent, learned, fascinating, and even spiritually helpful; but if it contains no reference at all to the central fact of Christ crucified, it is open to the charge of inadequacy and unfaithfulness'' (Mar. 13, 1964).

Philip Schaff, great church historian wrote: ''Without money and arms, Jesus Christ conquered more millions than Alexander, Caesar, Mohammed, and Napoleon; without science and learning, He shed more light on things human and divine than all the philosophers and scholars combined; without eloquence of the school, He spoke words of life such as were never spoken before, nor since, and produced effects which lie beyond the reach of orator or poet; without writing a single line, He has set more pens in motion and furnished themes for more sermons, orations, discussions, works of art, learned volumes, and sweet songs of praise than the whole army of great men of ancient and modern times.''

A number of societies exist to study the religions of the world. One such organization has on its official stationary a row of illustrations across the top of each sheet of letter paper. Each illustration in the series depicts the founder of one of the world's religions. The founders are shown in characteristic poses. Some are teaching or preaching. Others are wrapped in meditation. Only one is suffering. Only Jesus hangs on a cross.

1

The Word of Concern

And Jesus said, "Father, forgive them; for they know not what they do" (Luke 23:34, RSV*).*

Christian, in Bunyan's *Pilgrim's Progress,* toils along a lonely highway that is bounded on both sides by a stone wall. His back is bent beneath the burden of sin he bears. His steps are slow because his load is large and heavy. Finally he reaches the top of a hill. Here his way is blocked by a cross. Pilgrim gazes at the cross. As he looks, his heavy load drops from his back and rolls down the hill. Forgiven at the cross and relieved of his load of sin and guilt, Christian goes quickly and with great joy on his way. He begins to sing:

> Blest cross; blest sepulchre. Blest rather be
> The man that there was put to shame for me.

Bishop McDowell once said to a large gathering, "I would not go across the street to give India a new theology, India now has more theology than it can understand; or to give China a new code of ethics, China has a vastly better ethical code than ethical life; or to give Japan a new religious literature, Japan now has a better religious literature than religious life. But I would go across the world again and again, if it pleased God, to tell India and China and Africa of my experience at the cross.''

Like lightning our Lord's first words from the cross strike into the heart of all our trouble. How much we need the proper concept of God as a forgiving God! How much we need a proper understanding of forgiveness! How much we need a proper perspective of ourselves, both our inadequacy within ourselves, as well as what we can be in Christ!

Looking at the cross, we hear a voice cry out above the noise of confusion from the distance of twenty centuries. The cross supplies the answer to our need. Actually this prayer of Jesus was probably uttered not once but again and again, as the imperfect tense of the original verb indicates. At each indignity and invective, Jesus kept saying, ''Father, forgive them; for they know not what they do.''

The night of agony included betrayal, the garden experience where Jesus agonized all night in prayer, six successive mock trials, and the worst military flogging and taunting possible. While the executioners were putting Him through such an awful death that Roman law said no Roman citizen dare experience it, and while the nails were driven into His hands and feet, our Lord, true to His own teaching concerning forgiveness, asked forgiveness for the tormentors.

A Revelation of God's Nature

Eight of Christ's prayers are recorded in the Gospels. All but one are very brief. Most are single sentences. All of them address God as Father. Jesus, when He taught His disciples to pray, pointed out that true prayer begins with ''Our Father.''

''We are redeemed,'' said an ancient church father, ''when we receive a right view of God.'' And the first word from the cross throws its revealing light upon God Himself. It opens our eyes to see Him as He is. Yes, God is Creator, King, and Judge.

But He is more than all those things. He is Father. He is one who seeks, in all possible ways, to show us His love, concern, care, and compassion.

Jesus knew that the Father longs for the best in His children. He longs and loves so that He can forgive. The underlying cause for Christ's coming and for His crucifixion was to provide for our forgiveness. We can never lose sight of the forgiving Father as long as the cross lights up our moral darkness. At the cross we descend into the profoundest depth of love and desire. The first thing Jesus did on the cross was to place God in His true relation to us all, as a Father who loves and longs to save us. Christ did not call to God as Judge, but as Father.

Hans Egede, early missionary to Greenland, preached on the justice of God. After eight years he was still without a convert. He felt people must first know that God hates sin. As the text for his farewell sermon he chose the words, "I have worked for naught."

After Egede left Greenland, John Beck was sent there by the Moravian church. For his first text Beck used John 3:16, "For God so loved the world, that he gave his only begotten Son, that whosoever believeth in him should not perish, but have everlasting life."

At the close of the first service a chieftain asked him to repeat the text. He repeated it, and the chieftain asked him to repeat it again. Then the chieftain said, "That is a new kind of God. Our gods are gods of hate, not love." The chieftain accepted Christ and led his whole tribe in becoming Christians. It is the love back of the cross that is the motive the world wants to hear.

Calvary is a picture of God as a loving Father who gave His very best for us. And this word, "Father," spoken by Christ, revealed that His faith remained unshaken by all the suffering He endured. He had descended into a deeper desolation than anyone else could ever know. Yet still He continued to trust in His Father's provision and power.

It is easy to think of God as Father when all goes well, when the blessings of life are abundant, and when friends stand true by your side to support you. But our faith is strained because righteousness is trampled underfoot and evil seems on the throne, it is easy to question if a wise and loving Father really is in charge.

How beautiful, expressive, and unquestioning was the confidence Christ had in the Father amid His torture and agony! No wonder some said, "He trusted in God." In His difficult hour He did not question the wisdom and love of His Father.

When, in the early days of Christianity, the mob said to aged Polycarp as he faced the burning fagots, "Recant or die!" there was no futile debate or fearful hesitation on his part. Listen to this triumphant testimony from one who had experienced the Father's forgiveness in his own life. "Eighty and six years have I served Christ, and He has done me no harm; how could I now blaspheme my King who has redeemed me?" The flames claimed his flesh and the burning fagots dismembered his body, but they did not disturb his faith.

A Revelation of Christ's Mission

In the wonderful prophecy in Isaiah 53 at least ten statements are made about Jesus' humiliation and suffering. The prophet points out that the Messiah shall be despised and rejected of men. He shall be a man of sorrows and acquainted with grief. He will be wounded, bruised, and chastized. He will be led without resistance to the slaughter. He will be dumb like a lamb before his shearers. He will suffer at the hands of man. He will pour out his soul unto death. He will be buried in a tomb borrowed from a rich man. He will be numbered with the transgressors and He will make intercession for the transgressors.

How completely Christ fulfilled all that the prophet predicted. And in His first word from the cross, as He reached the climax of His suffering, He had no venom in His voice. He had no sarcasm in His speech. He had no wrath in His words.

This intercessory prayer for forgiveness, as perhaps no other sentence in the Gospels, embodies beautifully the spirit of Jesus.

Among the particulars foretold concerning Him is that which says He shall "make intercession for the transgressors." During His life He prayed for others. Now, at the cross that intercession continued. Before this He had prayed fervently for His disciples. Now the disciples whom He loved had deserted Him. The priests hated Him, the mobsters cried for His life, Pilate mishandled justice, and the soldiers were harsh to Him in His helplessness. The black sky brooding over Golgotha then has arched above all persons since. But Christ's pleas were in intercession for all of them—and for all of us.

In this prayer He anticipated His resurrection office of intercession. His eternal office as High Priest began at the cross. "There is one God, and there is one mediator between God and men, the man Christ Jesus" (1 Tim. 2:5, RSV). He is a "faithful high priest in things pertaining to God, to make reconciliation for the sins of the people" (Heb. 2:17). "He is able also to save them to the uttermost that come unto God by him, seeing he ever liveth to make intercession for them" (Heb. 7:25).

In His Sermon on the Mount, as in all His teaching, our Lord taught, "Love your enemies, bless them that curse you, do good to them that hate you, and *pray* for them which despitefully use you, and persecute you" (Matt. 5:44). That was the sermon *on* the mount. Now, in His sermon *from* the mount, in His word from the cross, what He taught was incarnate.

All His life He revealed God as a God of love and compassion. At the cross, rather than calling down curses upon His enemies, or calling upon waiting legions of angels to deliver Him, or throwing down threatening words upon His adversaries, He called upon God to be merciful to them; He begged God's forgiveness. He who taught His disciples to pray blessings upon their enemies, now prayed for His enemies.

Years ago in a Laymen's Missionary Convention, held in Chicago, a missionary told the story of a holy man in India. This holy man came to a Christian missionary to inquire what He was preaching. The missionary told him the story of Jesus' prayer, "Father, forgive them for they know not what they do." The holy man listened with increasing agitation. At the end of the story he sprang up and said, "Get out of here! Get out of India! You will convert all our people if you talk to them that way. In our religion we have no story of love like that."

At the cross we see better than anywhere else a picture of God. Not only did Jesus call Him Father, but, through the portrait of Christ on the cross, we see what kind of God He is and to what limits He will go to forgive. Edwin Markham wrote:

> Here is a truth in a little creed,
> Enough for all the roads we go;
> In love is all the law we need,
> And Christ is all the God we know.

For God so loved He gave. For God so loved He forgave. It is the character of God the Father to forgive. It is the way of Christ to forgive. And, as Sir John Seeley points out in *Ecce Homo,* when people speak of the "Christian Spirit" they usually mean a forgiving spirit.

A Revelation of Our Condition

Always the cross is a great revealer of ourselves. It reveals first of all our ignorance. Joseph Fort Newton once asserted in a sermon, "The stupidity of man causes as much suffering as his sin." Jesus interceded, saying, "They know not what they do." What? How can it be? Was not the crucifixion planned and purposeful? Was it not a premeditated occurrence? Yes, yes it was, and yet they didn't know what they were doing. Everyone of them was deceived. They were blinded and misinformed. They misunderstood. Envy led them down the wrong lane. Malice maddened them. The soldiers were just doing their duty.

Dr. Harry Emerson Fosdick described it this way: "That is

what man is capable of doing to the choicest soul that ever visited the earth. There the full measure of man's sin stands revealed, the abyss of baseness man can fall to. What a beast and devil man can be! How full of such barbarity his history is! How can one believe in man, hope anything from man, when one sees the cross as an exhibition of his stupidity and his pitiless cruelty unleashed through all his history upon the innocent?"

Sin is spiritual blindness. Sin gives a distorted sight, a view of duty and good which repels rather than reaches out. How often have we said of ourselves, "I don't know why I did it." In all our sin there is an element of spiritual stupidity. And forgiveness has the power to effect a cure for the blindness of sin. "They know not" are words which contain an excuse, a plea, in the face of the worst wickedness. It is as if Jesus was searching for a reason why God should forgive.

How Christ's words describe all those connected with His betrayal and death! Later Simon Peter included them all, especially, no doubt, the religious leaders, when he said at Pentecost, "You denied the Holy and Righteous One, and asked for a murderer to be granted to you. And now, brethren, I know that you acted in ignorance, as did also your rulers" (Acts 3:14, 17, RSV).

Yes, ignorance describes us all. If we were less blinded we could see how easily we raise the cross and crucify Christ afresh; how we put Him, time and again, to open shame. Theodore Heimarek says, "Deceived men crucified the Lord. They were not the kind of people we ordinarily call 'wicked' people. No, they were ordinary people with ordinary sinfulness. They were intensely interested in protecting personal security and institutions vital to their life. They argued it out with themselves and the people around them on the basis of community welfare and National safety."

In *Testament of Love,* Herbert L. Simpson says in referring to Christ's words, "That means that we are all a great deal worse than we can possibly realize. The Savior intercedes for us on the grounds that we have no idea whom we are hitting nor how hard we are hitting Him. We imagine we are only conforming to the level of all around us, doing what others are doing; not getting much satisfaction out of it, perhaps, as little as the soldiers got. They had no idea they were hitting God. It is at once the cause of forgiveness of our sin and the most awful experience of it" (p. 37, Nodder & Stroughton, 1934).

We crucify Christ in many ways. When we leave a desperate person to his despair, and abandon a lonely person in his loneliness; when we forsake a sorrowing one in his sorrow, we raise the cross of Christ again. When we refuse to forgive; and when we react against our suffering, by which we are united to Christ; we refuse Him. We refuse in ignorance when we refuse the cross given to us.

George Mattheson, the blind preacher and poet of Edinburgh, in one of his incomparable little prayers, says, "My God, I never thanked Thee for my thorns. I have thanked Thee a thousand times for my roses, but not once for my thorns. I have looked forward to a world when I shall get compensation for my cross, but I have never thought of my cross itself a present glory. Thou divine love, whose human path has been perfected through suffering, teach me to value my thorns, teach me to glory in my cross."

O Cross that lifteth up my head,
I dare not ask to fly from thee;
I lay in dust life's glory dead,
And from the ground there blossoms red
Life that shall endless be.

This prayer of our dying Lord, which was so harmonious with His life and is the embodiment of His teaching, is the pattern for us. The apostle Peter points out in First Peter 2:21-23, "For even hereunto were ye called: because Christ also suffered for us, leaving us an example, that ye should follow his steps: Who did not sin, neither was guile found in his mouth: Who, when he was reviled, reviled not again; when he suffered, he threatened not; but committed himself to him that judgeth righteously.''

So the voice of Christ on the cross calls down through the ages. It is the Christian's duty and calling to forgive, even as God for Christ's sake forgives us. We are not only to forgive those who have injured us, but we are to desire God's pardoning mercy for them. Even in death, love and forgiveness rise above hatred.

This great prayer from the Sermon on Mount Calvary brings forgiveness, and also constrains us to forgive. The cross, if understood at all, compels us, enables us, to forgive. At the cross our pride is broken and we see that we are to do more good unto others than they do unto us. We are to do unto others as God in Christ does unto us. And we do not forgive in the scriptural sense until we can pray, ''Father, forgive them, for they know not what they are doing.'' We do not really forgive until we desire God's forgiveness for all who may hurt or harm us.

How many, down through the centuries, have taken the way of Christ! And how glorious is their witness! Stephen, the first martyr, when stoned, ''kneeled down, and cried with a loud voice, Lord, lay not this sin to their charge'' (Acts 7:60). John Huss was a great martyr and forerunner of Luther. On July 6, 1415, in the city of Konstanz, Germany, while his flesh was slowly consumed by the cruel martyr fire, he cried ''Father, forgive them, for they know not what they do.''

Sir Thomas More, Lord Chancellor of England, was tried at Westminster and condemned to death without just cause. He said to his judges, ''As St. Paul held the clothes of those who stoned Stephen to death, and as they are both now saints in heaven, and shall continue there friends forever, so I verily trust, and shall, therefore most heartily pray, that though your Lordships have now here on earth been judges to my condemnation, we may nevertheless hereafter cheerfully meet in heaven in everlasting Salvation.''

We need to accept this intercessory work and sacrifice of Christ for us and believe that God does forgive us. Martin Luther wrote: "Whoever wavers and doubts whether his sins are forgiven does not trust in God and despairs of Christ, for he considers his sin greater and stronger than the death and blood of Jesus Christ."

We need also to realize that it is only as we forgive that we are forgiven. These are the words of the Master also. A sign that we have entered the family of the forgiven is that we now find it easy to forgive. The reason some people do not know the receiving of forgiveness is that they have not forgiven some other person. George Herbert wrote, "He that cannot forgive others, breaks the bridge over which he himself must pass if he would ever reach heaven; for every one has need to be forgiven." And isn't it striking that at the end of the great chapter 18 in Matthew, Jesus spoke of the unforgiving one being handed over to the tormentors. Few things bring greater torment physically, mentally, and spiritually than the attitude of unforgiveness.

To forgive those who wrong us and yet to hope somehow they will get their punishment from God or others, is not Christian forgiveness. To forgive those who treat us ill but *not* to pray God's forgiveness for them is still not Christ's love and forgiveness. To forgive those who destroy us and to plead God's pardon upon them is Christian forgiveness. Mark Twain once wrote: "Forgiveness is the fragrance the violet sheds on the heel that crushed it."

Jesus, after a powerful discussion on forgiveness in Matthew 18, followed this by a story of one who didn't forgive. He pointed out that the one who did not forgive was handed over to the tormentors. Whatever these tormentors might be, it is a known fact that much mental and physical illness falls upon unforgiving persons. Few things turn all life to bitterness, and health to illness, as an unforgiving spirit.

In a certain women's meeting, the subject for informal discussion turned to health and the cures of various illnesses. Finally a woman told how she was unable to sleep one night. She had a miserable headache. Late in the night she was rehearsing many things in her mind. One thing returned repeatedly. It was the hatred she had for a neighbor, whom she thought had wronged her. Finally the idea came to her, "If this woman has said harsh things against me, if they are true, I ought to appreciate it. And if they are wrong, it cannot hurt me and I ought to forgive her." She said, "I resolved right then and there to forgive her." My attitude of mind was changed; my headache left; I slept the remainder of the night. Taking this as a lesson, I have followed it. Every time I have a headache or feel disagreeable I try to find someone to forgive and I am relieved." She told how she found that whenever she exercised the attitude of forgiveness, her pains were fewer. She had not been sick for forty-five years. Hatred harms—forgiveness helps!

"Forgiveness," said John G. Chatalas, "is the hardest thing in the world. And because it is so difficult, it is a test of our character. Indeed it is the gauge of our Christian faith. The reason it is so difficult is that love is reaching from a minus point rather than from a neutral position. Loving someone whom we like or who likes us is sometimes difficult enough, but when we've been hurt—that's the test."

O wondrous love! O matchless Christ! You have indeed ushered in a new era. You have made the magnanimity of the soul the standard of true religion. Under the old order, "An eye for an eye and a tooth for a tooth," we might all make excellent Christians. We might be well nigh perfect. But now, looking at the cross, and hearing these words from the cross, how far short we fall!

Yet if we breathe not Your spirit, we are not Yours. If we practice not Your forgiveness, we are not Your disciples. If our hearts are hard and bitter against any who have wronged us, then we have failed, miserably failed, to understand this first word from Calvary!

How hardly man this lesson learns,
To smile and bless the hand that spurns,
To see the blow, to feel the pain,
To render only love again!
One had it—but He came from heaven,
Reviled, rejected, and betrayed;
No curse He breathed, no plaint He made,
But when in death's dark pang He sighed,
Prayed for His murderers, and died.
—Author unknown

Forgiven? Yes! It is the password of the Christian.

2

The Word of Compassion

To day shalt thou be with me in paradise.

† † †

† † † † †

Janet Kreider in *The Way of the Cross and Resurrection* tells of Larry Lehman, a missionary in Guatemala. He came in contact with a man from Chitana whom people feared because of his great strength. One day this man met Christ in conversion. Soon after he believed, however, disastrous things began to happen. Not only did his cow die mysteriously, but his pig and dog died also. He was ostracized by his community. His life and the lives of his family were threatened.

These trials drew the man from Chitana nearer to the Lord. And the Spirit of Christ removed hate and anger from his heart. He was filled with love for those who mistreated him. Thirty-five people from his country came to faith also.

In an effort to destroy him, fifteen men drew up a paper under oath, saying that he had removed images from the local church and burned them. The authorities soon saw the falsehoods and acquitted him.

Next the judge sought to prosecute the accusers for perjury, but the man from Chitana, who had previously fought all who threatened him, pleaded for the judge to pardon his enemies. The judge granted his request. Within a year the believers numbered 135 (pp. 134–135, Herald Press, 1978).

2

The Word of Compassion

"To day shalt thou be with me in paradise" (Luke 23:43).

In the first word, or statement, from the cross the Savior asked for pardon. In the second, He granted pardon. The first word is a priestly prayer; the second is a royal pardon. The first is a plea for forgiveness; the second is a pledge for salvation.

Always Christ was full of compassion. He demonstrated His compassion to the sick, the leper, the widow, the poor, the simple, and those without a Shepherd. In this second word from the cross Christ continued to demonstrate His complete compassion. This is one of the most dramatic scenes in the Scripture.

The Picture

As we look at Calvary we see three crosses. With Jesus, the Scripture tells us, were crucified two thieves, one on His right hand and the other on His left. Rome found it practical to conduct a multiple crucifixion because it saved time and money. And the punishment was always a reminder of Rome's power.

To associate Christ with criminals in His death was the final touch of indignity and disgrace. Yet these robbers furnish one of the most pathetic and provocative incidents in the entire Gospel story. In several sentences the story of salvation is written. And the response of mankind is recorded. Placed between two thieves was no accident, for Christ changed that crowning touch of cruelty into the sublimest picture of confession and compassion.

Isaiah's prophecy was exact. "He was numbered with the transgressors and he made his grave with the wicked in his death." And the phrase, "the one on his right hand and the other on his left," is a phrase Christ used again and again. When popularity surrounded Jesus and prosperity seemed to be in the wind, when the kingdom appeared to be near, the mother of James and John came petitioning Jesus, "Grant that my sons may sit the one on your right hand and the other on the left, when you come into your kingdom." Jesus, in an obvious reference to the cross said, "You don't know what you are asking. Are you able to drink the cup I'm going to drink of?" "Yes, we are able," they answered. But where were these petitioners at the cross?

We find the phrase used again in Matthew 25, where Christ is speaking of the final judgment of the nations. He will separate the sheep from the goats, the sheep on the right hand and the goats on the left. Now, at the cross, with Jesus between two wicked criminals whom the law said deserved crucifixion, we find the phrase again.

Further, the Gospel writer pictures others around the cross and what they were saying. "The chief priests mocking him, with the scribes and elders, said, He saved others; himself he cannot save. If he be the King of Israel, let him now come down from the cross, and we will believe him. He trusted in God; let him deliver him now, if he will have him: for he said, I am the Son of God. The thieves also, which were crucified with him, cast the same in his teeth" (Matt. 27:41–44).

But something happened and the picture was different. One thief changed his outlook. Was it when, time after time Jesus prayed for God to forgive His crucifiers, that the thief came to believe something different of this Christ? Was it the sign written above the cross? Was it because the behavior of Jesus was so different? The picture in Scripture says that the one thief rebuked the other for railing, saying "Dost not thou fear God, seeing thou art in the same condemnation? And we indeed justly; for we receive the due reward of our deeds: but this man hath done nothing amiss. And he said unto Jesus, Lord, remember me when thou comest into thy kingdom" (Luke 23:40–42).

The Pardon

At the beginning, both robbers denounced Christ. Then one repented. These words reveal a complete change in the thief's attitude toward his fellow-men, his past life, his crimes, his punishment, and Christ.

"That his repentance was sincere," says Charles R. Erdman, "appears (1) in that he regarded his crimes not merely as offences against man, but as defiance against God; he cried to the other robber, 'Dost thou not fear God?' (2) He admits that his punishment is deserved, 'We indeed (are condemned) justly; for we receive the due reward of our deeds.' (3) Repentance involves a change of conduct, and the penitent robber is heard rebuking his former comrade in crime.

"The faith of the robber is even more remarkable. He regards Christ as a Savior, and as a coming King: 'Lord, remember me when thou comest in thy kingdom.' Such an expression of submission and trust is of the very essence of faith" (*Remember Jesus Christ*, p. 93–94, Eerdmans Pub. Co., Grand Rapids).

John Calvin wrote: "I know not that, since the creation of the world, there ever was a more remarkable and striking example of faith . . . how acute must have been the eyes of his mind, by which he beheld life in death, exaltation in ruin, glory in shame, victory in destruction, a kingdom in bondage."

"Surely," says Ronald S. Wallace, "this is where we must all begin again, if we are to be given the eyes to see and the power to repent—with the trembling of one who knows he cannot live apart from God, and who never ceases to cry out 'Jesus, remember me!' We, too have to be brought to the point where we cease to justify ourselves, and admit that whatever has come to us in life as a result of our folly and sin is much less than the 'dire reward of our deeds!' Here, where faith and repentance begin, the pity of God is always ready to begin again'' (p. 29, *Words of Triumph*, John Knox Press, Richmond, Va., 1964).

Synesius of Cyrene, at the beginning of the fifth century, wrote words which remind us of the repentant thief.

Lord Jesus, think on me,
And purge away my sin;
From earthborn passions set me free,
And make me pure within.

Lord Jesus, think on me,
With care and woe oppressed;
Let me Thy loving servant be,
And taste Thy promised rest.

Lord Jesus, think on me,
That when the flood is past,
I may th'eternal brightness see,
And share Thy joy at last.

''Remember me.'' These words, like the publican's short and simple prayer, mean so much. And the cross did not paralyze Christ's pardoning power. Rather the cross intensified it, magnified it, glorified it, and sanctified it. For always when true penitence is present, pardon is present also. Christ ''breaks the power of cancelled sin and sets the prisoner free.''

At first glance we find in this thief and his prayer only a flickering faith that forced his halting words. His faith was not impressive. But thanks be to God, we are not saved by the greatness of our faith, nor by the nobility of our lives, nor by the heroism of our death. There is salvation for the thief and for each of us because, on that grim, skull-shaped mount of execution, God's grace in Christ was abundant. And when the mumbled words of a dying thief fell on Jesus' ears, all the resources of divine love responded in Christ's glorious reply. "Verily I say unto thee, to day shalt thou be with me in paradise."

If we look only at the weak and dying thief to understand salvation, we will fail miserably. If we look for a clue to his deliverance in that wasted and doomed life we will not find one. The real clue is the love of God, which always goes far beyond our greatest expectations. It awakens our stunned, sin and pain-stricken senses with joy and gladness. The emphasis is not on the quantity or quality of the thief's faith, but on the gracious, compassionate love of Jesus.

Christ is so eager to save us that He senses our slightest move in His direction. His love looks so deep and longs so for our salvation that He responds to the smallest request with superabundant aid.

C. S. Lewis writes concerning his own conversion in his book *Surprised by Joy*: "You must picture me alone in that room in Magdalen, night after night, feeling whenever my mind lifted even for a second from my work, the steady, unrelenting approach of Him whom I so earnestly desired not to meet. That which I greatly feared had at last come upon me. In the Trinity Term of 1929 I gave in, and admitted that God was God, and knelt and prayed: perhaps, that night, the most dejected and reluctant convert in all England. I did not then see what is now the most shining and obvious thing; the Divine humility which will accept a convert on such terms. The Prodigal Son at least walked home on his own feet. But who can duly adore that love which will open the high gates to a prodigal who is brought in knocking, struggling, resentful and darting his eyes in every direction for a chance to escape? The words *'compelle intrare,'* compell them to come in, have been so abused by wicked man that we shudder at times; but, properly understood, they plumb the depth of Divine mercy. The hardness of God is kinder than the softness of men, and His compulsion is our liberation."

Let the meaning of all this filter into our souls until we learn the astonishing fact that Jesus saves miserable, wretched, lost sinners who have nothing to offer; until we see that we are no better than the thief. If we are proud and think God saves us because we are no worse than many and better than most, we have never been to Calvary. As long as we keep fooling ourselves this way, we have no hope. It is when we see that in deserving salvation we are no different from the thief that we can hear Christ's word of pardon. For when we lay our lives beneath the sharp light in God's holiness, we discover that our jealousies, our hatreds, our prejudices, our dishonesty, and our lust are all an abomination in the sight of God. All of us, no matter how respected, must call for God's mercy. And when we do, His mercy is abundant.

> There is a fountain filled with blood
>   Drawn from Emmanuel's veins;
> And sinners plunged beneath that flood
>   Lose all their guilty stains.
> The dying thief rejoiced to see
>   That fountain in his day;
> And then may we, though vile as he,
>   Wash all our sins away.

The Promise and Presence

"Today, you shall be *with me* in paradise." "With me," Jesus had said of the future state, when praying for His disciples in John 17. "With me," Jesus repeated to the dying thief. The burden of the words is not on the location of Paradise, but on the pardon and presence of Christ. "Where Jesus is 'tis heaven." What an inspiring thought! After death we are at once ushered into the presence of Jesus. Paul the apostle wrote: "To be absent from the body is to be present with the Lord."

Richard Baxter put it this way:

> My knowledge of that life is small;
> The eye of faith is dim;
> But 'tis enough that Christ knows all,
> And I shall be with Him.

For the dying, penitent thief there was life in that look to Jesus. There was life in the plea, "Jesus, remember me."

One stormy Sunday, Spurgeon entered a primitive little Methodist chapel in Colchester, England. A local pastor was preaching to a dozen or fifteen persons. The preacher repeated the text with hesitant pronunciation, "Look unto me and be ye saved, all the ends of the earth." The pastor preached on the simple text in a homely fashion for a few minutes. Then with the freedom of a less conventional age than ours, he looked straight at the young stranger in the congregation and said, "Young man, you look very miserable, miserable in life and miserable in death, if you don't obey my text; but if you obey now, this moment you will be saved. Young man, look to Jesus Christ, look. You have nothing to do but to look and live."

Today a visitor to the little chapel may read on a tablet these words, "Near this spot C. H. Spurgeon looked and lived." At that place began one of the greatest ministries of the centuries. That was the fountainhead of the mighty man of God from whom people in all parts of the world drank and were refreshed.

Two criminals were equally close to the cross. Each saw and heard all that transpired for six long hours. Both were wicked. Both were suffering. Both were dying and both needed forgiveness. Yet one died in his sins. The other found forgiveness and a future with Christ.

Under the same sermon some hear and respond with indifference. Others' eyes are opened to their need, move close to Christ, and cry for mercy. It is not a question of Christ's desire or ability to forgive. Why should one person in the presence of light still be content to choose darkness? Why does the cross harden one and soften another? Why does the sun melt ice and harden clay? Why is the cross for some the gateway to heaven and for others the door to hell?

Two robbers died equally close to Christ. One was saved, the other lost. As an old English pastor put it years ago: "One was saved and therefore no one should despair; yet only one, and therefore no one should presume."

Salvation and judgment are in the cross. All through Scripture salvation and judgment are joined. Even in that great salvation Scripture of John 3:16 we have salvation and judgment pointed out as the two possibilities for all people, "For God so loved the world, that he gave his only begotten Son, that whosoever believeth in him should not perish, but have everlasting life."

Never has the story of the dying thief encouraged a person to procrastinate, or to dally with his destiny, or to delay a decision for Christ. When a person says regarding salvation, as a kind of excuse for not receiving Christ now, "There is hope for me. Remember the thief on the cross," it is perfectly proper to ask, "Which thief do you want me to remember?"

This thief's words were words of faith, not of fear, as are many deathbed conversions. Many times, to those who wait, prayer seems strange and God's love foreign. The hour of death has in itself no power to awaken a sense of guilt or to lead to salvation. Remember Shakespeare, who says—

> Try what repentance can, what can it not?
> And yet, what can it when it cannot repent!

Andrew W. Blackwood wrote: "I have been with several hundred people during the course of their last few hours or days on earth. With many of these friends I have discussed what lies beyond. I can report that those who face the future with Christ look forward with hope, while those who enter the uncertainties of death without Him show at best a brave resignation, at worst a sickening, heartbreaking fear. We have a faith that teaches us to die in the confidence that our Lord keeps His promises. Even more our faith teaches us how to live'' (p. 27–28, *The Voice From the Cross,* Baker Book House, Grand Rapids, 1955).

Let us not compliment ourselves on the merit of our faith in Christ. Rather let us be grateful to Him for His faith in us, and for the gracious rewards He prepares for our feeble faith.

We marvel not at the merit of this man's faith, but at the magnitude of our Lord's forgiveness. Through grace the dying thief, who had not lived for Christ or given any service in Christ's kingdom, became a forgiven and redeemed sinner fit for paradise. That is grace. And it is only grace which gives us a place in the Lord's presence.

Thank God for those who have in a sober, thoughtful, clear moment accepted Christ. Better to approach the throne of compassion when life, not death, is upon us. Yes, the thief received a pardon in the last moments of life. How much better to receive the pardon when life beckons to service and sacrifice, to devotion and daring!

''The cross,'' said William Barclay, ''is the proof that there is no length to which the love of God will refuse to go in order to win men's hearts. The cross is the medium of reconcilation because the cross is the final proof of the love of God; and a love like that demands an answering love.''

The blind poet George Matheson wrote:

> O cross that liftest up my head,
> I dare not ask to fly from thee;
> I lay in dust life's glory dead,
> And from the ground there blossoms red
> Life that shall endless be.

3

The Word of Care

Woman, behold thy son!
Behold thy mother!

† † †

† † † † †

George Eliot says in her novel *Felix Holt,* "'Tis a great and mysterious gift, this clinging of the heart, whereby it hath often seemed to me that, even in the very moment of suffering, souls have the keenest foretaste of heaven. I speak not lightly, but as one who has endured. And 'tis a strange truth that only in the agony of parting we look into the depths of love."

† † †

An old legend teaches us that Christ is dependent upon us to share the message of the cross with others. It says that when Jesus had completed his work on earth, the angel Gabriel asked Him, "What plan do you have for carrying on your work? How will others know what you did?" Jesus replied, "I left it for Peter and James and John and Martha and Mary, to tell their friends, and their friends to tell their friends, until the whole world hears." To this Gabriel asked, "But suppose they fail? Suppose Peter is so busy with nets and Martha is full of her housework, or the friends they tell are so occupied that they forget to tell? What is your plan then?" Jesus replied, "I have no other plan. I am counting on them."

The Word of Care

"When Jesus therefore saw his mother, and the disciple standing by, whom he loved, he saith unto his mother, Woman, behold thy son! Then saith he to the disciple, Behold thy mother! And from that hour that disciple took her into his own home"
(John 19:26–27).

Years ago, according to Edward Jeffries Rees, a large number of Americans were serving in foreign service when a strange and terrible eye disease seized many of them. A mother discovered that her small son had the disease, which, within a few days after the appearance of the first symptoms, would cause her child to become totally blind. The child, unaware of the seriousness of his condition, followed his mother into the garden and obeyed her instructions.

His mother said, "See the sun. Look at it. See its light—wonderful sunlight!" Her small son squinted his eyes and endeavored to look into the face of the burning sun. Then his mother took him over to a beautiful rose bush, filled with red roses. She picked one and gave it to her child. "Hold it, my son," she said. "It is a beautiful rose. See its tender petals. Smell its fragrance—roses, roses, son, red roses!" Then she lifted her son into her arms saying, "Look at your mother's face, son! What color is my hair? Look at my eyes. What color are they?" She drew her son close to her, held him tightly and looked lovingly into his upturned eyes. "Now what do you see in your mother's eyes, son?" The little boy replied, "I see love, Mother, I see love." The vision of sunlight and the rose and the face of his mother remained in the memory of her son, who was soon blind. But most of all he remembered the look of love.

What remains in our minds about Calvary? It is the word love. Christ lived in love. And here, on the cross, we see love in the face of Jesus. We see love on the face of Mary. We see love on the face of the beloved disciple John. It was a radiant and reciprocal love. It was a love which cared. And love cared so much that, in the midst of the greatest suffering the mind and body can endure, it saw the concern of others and sought to meet another's need. This is the key to the meaning of the fourth phrase of Christ from Calvary. It is Christ's demonstration of divine love for His mother and for all in need. The third word, or assertion, from the cross, along with the first two, carry concern for others.

In an old book, *Voices of the Passion,* the author suggests that the first word of the cross marches upward toward heaven and transforms the cross into the flaming altar of the world's High Priest: "Father, forgive them for they know not what they do." He suggests that the second word transforms Calvary into the vestibule of heaven and the open door to eternity: "Today shalt thou be with me in paradise."

The third word, however, remains here on earth. It opens the heart to human love. Here is the perfect blending of human affection and divine glory; human tenderness, kindness, and care are coupled with divine truth and love.

The Scene

For a moment now we lose sight of the multitude. The robbers on either side seem silent. It is as if only three persons were present; the Master, the mother, and the most loved disciple, John. The sneering Pharisee, the vulgar mob, the gambling soldiers could not keep such people away. The poet Kipling surely had this scene of mother love in mind when he wrote:

> If I were hanged on the highest hill,
> I know whose love would follow me still,
> Mother o' mine, Mother o' mine.

Now Christ looks down at the foot of the cross. His feverish eyes find familiar faces. There, surrounded by the mocking multitude, the shuffling scoffer, and the hardened soldiers He sees His closest friends among His foes.

What a flood of recollection it must have brought! Surely Christ saw again, in a flash, the home in Nazareth. He heard, in His memory, His mother singing her lullaby to Him. He could feel the warmth and love of her arms as she held Him. Her words of guidance and comfort gave Him the strength of youth. All must have come back in moments.

There can be no doubt that Jesus loved His mother, not only through the first thirty years, but also during the eventful three years of His public ministry. The Gospel of John opens with the home scene at Cana of Galilee where Jesus and His mother stood side by side. John's Gospel closes with the scene of Jesus' mother standing by the cross while He gives direction concerning her future care. Although Christ did not allow filial love to turn Him aside from the path God had for Him, yet divine duty did not become a dodge for the exercise of filial love.

Three times Mary came into the public life of Jesus. First was at the wedding feast in Cana of Galilee; second, while He spoke to the multitude; and third, at this, His crucifixion.

"Now there stood by the cross his mother." What a flood of

memories must have passed in the mind of Mary. Undoubtedly she pondered the silent and holy night when her son was born in Bethlehem. She remembered the flight into Egypt to save His life. Once Mary heard the promise concerning her son; "He shall be great, and shall be called the Son of the Highest: and the Lord God shall give unto him the throne of his father David: and he shall reign over the house of Jacob for ever; and of his kingdom there shall be no end" (Luke 1:32–33). How can that promise ever be fulfilled?

Did Mary remember the prophecy of the devout Simeon when Jesus was presented as a baby in the temple? Old Simeon waited for the consolation of Israel. He took the baby Jesus up in his arms and blessed Him. He also said, "Lord, now lettest thou thy servant depart in peace, according to thy word: For mine eyes have seen thy salvation, Which thou hast prepared before the face of all people: A light to lighten the Gentiles, and the glory of thy people, Israel" (Luke 2:29–32). Then Simeon turned to Mary with the dark and ominous words, "Behold, this child is set for the fall and rising of many in Israel: and for a sign which shall be spoken against; (Yea, a sword shall pierce through your own soul also,) and the thoughts of many hearts shall be revealed" (Luke 2:34–35).

Mary was at the cross. And who can imagine what she went through? She felt every hammer's blow. She flinched under the prick of the thorn. She shuddered when the spear point pierced the side of her son. She was moved by the mocking crowd. In a real way His cross was also her cross.

Now Mary's son was dying and she could not help. His wounds were bleeding and she dare not take care of them. His mouth was parched, yet Mary was not allowed to moisten His lips. The nails held Him to the cross, but she may not loose them. How much Mary must have suffered!

Mary had kissed, so many times, the forehead, now torn with thorns. Not only the physical suffering, but every taunt, touched the tenderest spot of her heart and spirit. Every word spoken was a stab of pain for her as it was for Jesus. Mary, at the foot of the cross, was experiencing to the full the prophecy of Simeon. And Jesus knew, as no one else, her suffering. Her complete helplessness, in the face of His need, made His burden all the more unbearable.

When the supreme hour struck, Mary stood by the cross. Try as we might we cannot read fully the thoughts and emotions of Mary's heart. Christ's disciples had deserted Him. Friends had forsaken Him. His mother stood by His side. And not a word is recorded by any of the Gospels that she spoke. She suffered in unbroken silence. But she stood by the cross in transcendent courage. Hers was the greatest of privileges in bearing the Messiah. Hers was also the greatest of sorrows in seeing Him crucified.

At the cross her station keeping
Stood the mournful mother weeping,
  Where He hung, her dying Lord;
For her soul, of joy bereaved,
Bowed with anguish, deeply grieved,
  Felt the sharp and piercing sword.

The Statement

Jesus addressed His mother, "Woman, behold your son." For a long time I wondered at what seemed to be a crude address by Jesus to His mother. Why didn't He use the term "Mother"? Did He, as many write and speak concerning this word, want her to know that when it came to the grace of salvation, she stood with all others? Was it, as some declare, that Jesus wanted to impress upon His mother that suffering and pain must also be hers and cannot be avoided even by the Savior's mother? Was it, as still others point out, similar to former experiences, such as the time she asked Him for help at the wedding, and the time she waited in the crowd. Was He seeking to withdraw as her son so that she might see Him as her Savior—robbing her of her son so that she could see the Son of God? Was His word such, as still others suggest, that she may see her own salvation and the salvation of the whole world contained in the death of God's Son?

All these and others leave a void in my understanding of Jesus word, "Woman," in addressing His mother. Finally I am helped when I learn that this word, which Jesus used each time after He left His home, in the original language is a word of endearing respect. Marcus Dodds points out that this word is often used to address a queen, or a person of great distinction. It is also a term of separation. After Jesus embarks on His public ministry He never again calls Mary mother, but always this word of respect, honor, and separation. So it identified His respect and honor, as well as implying a difference in relationship. The care for His mother was characteristic of all His conduct.

"Son, behold your mother." And from that hour John took Mary to his own home. Love also brought John to Calvary. Love wishes to be present, to be near no matter what the cost. His soul was knit to the Savior. And to love his Lord was to love those whom the Lord loved. John loved Mary and stood by her when her other sons did not believe, when she stood grieving at the death of her oldest son, all other friends having forsaken her.

Nuncassy, the great artist, in his famous painting, "Christ on Calvary," represents John standing quietly, thoughtfully, and reverantly beside the cross. He is looking down upon the prostrate form of Mary. His face is calm and composed, yet it bears the signs of unmistakable sorrow. His affection seems to be divided between the Savior on the cross and Mary at the foot of the cross. His attitude seems to be an invitation to the dying Christ to confide in him, and Christ asks John to become a son to His mother, to fill His place in her life. How much like Christ John must have been! He shall become the son of consolation.

And John accepted this last legacy of love from his Lord. Mary went to live with John, where he and she could continue to comfort one another with the memories of Galilee, Jerusalem, and Judea. The two most dear were to help each other. She was to be to him a mother, and he was to be to her a son. From her John would learn much. He would learn the details of the birth and early life of our Lord.

The Precept

Religious faith cannot be divorced from the human life. If religious faith, the divine kind, is real, it is concerned about where we live and our suffering, about Christ and those who are in His care. Christ does not sever the bonds of family and of love for others. He does call for the highest loyalty and love for Himself, which gives more meaning to human love than any mere attachment to family alone can give.

How often we have seen it. A person yields fully, surrenders completely to Christ, putting Him before father and mother and all else. Then the glorious thing happens. Mother and father and all else are seen in their proper perspective. They are loved more than ever because they were loved by the Lord to the extent that He died for each. As a great saint of several centuries ago said, "The more I love Christ the more I love my wife."

So, in the act of redeeming the world, Jesus took time to make a special provision for His own aging mother. Given to the beloved and obedient disciple was the task of taking the very place of Christ to a wounded and broken soul. It is the highest privilege life can afford to stand in Christ's stead. One of the most comforting messages of the cross, and the misery and mystery of it, is that Christ's eye was not dimmed by the presence of His loved ones standing by. In the midst of untold suffering, He did not forget the woman who bore Him and the disciple who loved Him so much.

In this third word from the cross, our Lord tells us what Christian love means. It is neither a vaporous sentiment nor a matter of romantic emotion. It is the practical expression of thoughtful kindness in meeting immediate human needs. In the cruel suffering of the cross Christ remembered to express His gratitude and care.

While it is true that our faith reaches beyond the stars, it must be practiced on the surface of the earth right where we are. Some find it easy to be thoughtful of those who live in the Congos of our world, and to pray fervently for the salvation of souls who are a thousand miles away. This is, of course, an essential part of our faith. But it will never take the place of love for those who are close at hand. Global love is vast and important but it is dangerously impersonal. Our love is proven when we minister to the next person we meet who is in need.

Phillips Brooks was a spiritual giant and greatly loved pastor. Shortly after his death his oldest brother said to Dr. McVicker, "Phillip might have saved himself, and so prolonged his live. Others do; but he was always giving himself to any one who wanted him." Then Dr. McVicker answered, "Yes indeed! He might have saved himself, but in doing so, he would not have been Phillips Brooks. The glory of his life was that he did not save himself." And that is the secret of Christ's caring love.

As one has written, "The Christian religion is not only a religion of great churches, chanting choirs, and soaring cathedrals. It is a religion of the home and kitchen, of the little things of life. There is nothing on earth which it does not touch."

Those who love Christ care for those about whom Christ is concerned. John, the great lover of Jesus and the one whom, in a special way, Jesus loved, took care of the mother of his Master. To love as Christ loved is to see the seed beneath the dirty brown earth and know that in His love it can blossom forth into a beautiful flower.

A social worker was showing a woman from the suburbs through a poor tenement part of the city. The woman saw an especially dirty child. "Doesn't the mother love the child?" asked the woman of the social worker. "Yes," replied the worker, "the mother loves the child but doesn't hate dirt. I'm afraid you hate the dirt but don't love the child."

How easy it is to see the sinner and to fail to care as Christ cared.

We are sure also that Christ comprehends our sorrow and suffering. Who can doubt that He feels for us when a sword pierces our own hearts? The Lord is able to fill the vacant places of our lives. The separations which are so hard to understand are part of the progressive development of the whole.

So the brokenhearted company, gathered around the sinless one on the cross, is, in a real sense, representative of the great company, which no one can number, who suffer because of the sins of others—parents who suffer shame because of their children, for whom they would gladly die; the wife who suffers because of her husband's ill fate; and the husband who suffers because of his wife's sorrow.

Christ's love storms the gates of Heaven and pours itself into every nook and corner of life. Whatever our needs, no matter how abundant they are, all these we can bring to Him who in Calvary remembered His mother. He will also remember our needs. He knows and cares for those broken by sorrow, sin, anxiety, and care.

> The healing of the seamless dress
> Is by our beds of pain;
> We touch Him in life's throng and press
> And we are whole again.

4

The Word of Consolation

My God, my God, why hast thou forsaken me?

† † †

† † † † †

A beautiful illustration of the power of Christ through His cross is offered in the account of the erection of a mammoth monument of "The Christ of the Andes." In 1905 it seemed that war was about to break out between Chile and the Argentine Republic. Christian men and women fasted, prayed, and worked to avoid this calamity, and to maintain peace.

As a result of their efforts, war was avoided and a settlement of peace was made. Their guns were melted and made into a great statue, representing Christ, the Prince of Peace, as He stood at the base of a mighty cross. It was erected on top of the Andes Mountain boundary line. On the base of the monument are chiseled the words: "Sooner shall these mountains crumble into the dust than the Argentines and Chilians break the peace to which they have pledged themselves at the feet of Christ, the Redeemer."

† † †

Madame Chiang Kai-shek tells the story of a farmer who became a hero during an earthquake. His farm was on high land. As he looked down into the valley to the shoreline, he saw that the earthquake was causing the ocean to pile up. A tidal wave would soon leap upon the lowland. He realized that his neighbors below would perish unless he could call them immediately to his hilltop. Quickly he put a torch to his dry rice barn and rang the fire gong.

The people looked up and saw the smoke rising. They rushed up the hill to help fight the fire. But even before they had reached the burning barn, they heard the roar of the waves below, covering the fields they had just left. Immediately they knew that their neighbor had burned all his possessions in order to save their lives.

4

The Word of Consolation

And at the ninth hour Jesus cried with a loud voice . . . "My God, my God, why hast thou forsaken me?" (Mark 15:34).

In the National Gallery of Art hangs a unique painting of Calvary. The figure of Christ on the cross is almost hidden in the darkness. At first glance one sees nothing but the dim figure of the suffering Savior. But as one looks longer and with closer care, one sees another figure behind the Savior, with outstretched arms, tenderly supporting the suffering One. The face of the One holding is twisted by even more pain than the One crucified. In this way the artist seeks to show that God, the Father, is grieving and suffering with His Son, as He dies upon the cross.

Although it is impossible to explain all that these words from the cross mean, and although we cannot interpret all, we know that Christ experienced absolute abandonment, desertion, and loneliness. He reached the extremity of mental and spiritual agony, which brought a greater suffering than even the worst physical suffering. Not only had all His friends forsaken Him but now He felt forsaken even by the Father, God Himself.

Here at the cross Jesus endured the final and ultimate suffering, so that we need never experience such suffering. Here was utter loneliness, so that we need never experience complete separation. Here was abandonment by God, so that we need never be forsaken. Here was condemnation in our stead, so that we need never live unforgiven or guilty. Christ was forsaken by God so that the redeemed might be reconciled to God.

"As we examine the history of interpretation of this word in Christendom during the past two thousand years, we meet repeated attempts to escape from the stark horror of this word and to flee from it. Some say: Jesus spoke this word for us; for He was never forsaken by God, but we were (theophylact). Others say: Jesus does not pray for Himself, but in place of the Jews, whom God has forsaken since they have crucified Jesus. Or, the forsakenness applies only to Jesus' body (Thomas Aquinas). Again others say: When Jesus said 'My God, my God, why hast Thou forsaken me?' He did not think primarily of the beginning of Psalm 22, but of the whole Psalm, and in this Psalm we also read: 'The meek shall eat and be satisfied; they shall praise the Lord that sees Him' (verse 26). And finally Scheiermacher says: 'We may safely conclude from the application which the Savior made of this holy hymn to Himself . . . that also in this moment . . . He thought and felt about His death as clearly and calmly as we find Him doing everywhere in those last addresses by which He sought to prepare His disciples for His death" (p. 31, *The Victor Speaks*, by Edmund Schlink, Concordia).

The Darkness of Utter Loneliness

The first three times Christ spoke from the cross were during the first three hours. Now complete darkness descends and three more hours pass when not a word is even whispered, and Jesus suffers in silence. Silence and loneliness are harder to bear than open opposition, overwork, or ill health. Human nature needs sympathy and companionship, especially in difficult hours.

Darkness also increases agony. It is enough to be alone. But to be alone for three hours of total darkness! During the night, evil aligns its forces and attacks the sufferer. I recall so well, during a recent season of suffering, that I came to dread the night. I could tolerate and live during the day. But I dreaded the discouragement which so often settled in during the darkness of the night. How much more Jesus must have suffered, when not only the darkest day of history descended, but even the sense of the Father's presence left. The one who spoke so much of the Father's presence with Him and His being one with the Father was now left alone.

A small child was disobedient and for this her mother punished her by sending her to her room. After a short time the small one became lonely. She called repeatedly to her mother, asking that she be allowed to leave her room. But her mother did not answer. In desperation the small one finally called, "Please, Mother. Please take me back again. Please take me back." She sensed, at least to a small degree, the loneliness of separation.

How much more the Savior suffered in utter loneliness when not only His friends forsook Him, but even God forsook Him.

True, we cannot understand *what* He suffered. We can only begin to grasp *why* He suffered. And Calvary means that Christ entered so completely into our condition that He knows our ultimate misery: separation from God. He entered more deeply than we can ever know. He knew a separation inconceivable to us because He knew an intensity of closeness with God we do not know. And we stand amazed at the depth He went for us.

Elizabeth Barrett Browning sought to capture the story, the mystery and meaning, in her moving lines:

Deserted! God could separate from his own essence rather;
And Adam's sins have swept between the righteous Son and Father;
It went up single, echoless, "My God, I am forsaken!"
It went up from his holy lips, amid his lost creation
That no believer e'er should use those words of desolation!

The Darkness of Utter Separation

After Christ had hung on the cross, in writhing pain for three long hours, darkness descended. Such darkness came that it shut out the noonday sun. It was as if all nature sympathized with the suffering, and bore witness to the intense darkness of this day in human history, and this day in Christ's life. Now the experience of Jesus reached its darkest hour.

Such suffering was more than discouragement, depression, disillusionment, or despair. He demonstrated as completely as possible the utter separation which sin brings between humanity and God. Sin separates from God, and Christ upon the cross, bearing the sins of the world, bore to the nth degree all that separation. Christ endured the final tragedy of sin in human life, which is separation from God.

All of us have known, if we are spiritually sensitive, the separation which one sin will bring into a relationship. And we know that sin, above all, breaks the relationship with God. How much must be the Holy One's sense of separation when on Him was laid the sins of the whole world? How much agony must one, who was without sin, experience when God is separated and silent? How great must be the pain separation brings to the one who knew perfectly the Father's moment-by-moment companionship?

Terrible as physical suffering on the cross must have been, we obscure the true significance of the cross if we dwell too much on the physical side alone. Others probably have experienced physical suffering to the same extent. None certainly experienced the same anguish of soul and mind which makes the soul desolate and hopeless.

The good news of the cross is that Christ bore the ultimate separation which sin brings so that we need never be separated from God, from His help in our hour of need, or from His companionship here and hereafter.

But Light for Us

Because our Savior, who knew no sin, became sin for us and bore the complete price, the life of the believer is changed from darkness to light, from death to life, from utter despair and desolation to hope and consolation.

We cannot comprehend even a little of what the cross means without our hearts overflowing in gratitude and praise. We do not understand the cross without coming to a deeper commitment to the Christ of the cross.

Count Zinzendorf, famed leader of the Moravians, as a young man, saw a picture of Jesus upon the cross. Below the picture were the words, "Lo! This I have done for thee." This led to the conversion of Zinzendorf. Beneath the picture also were the words, "What hast thou done for me?" This second phrase led him to consecrate his life, wealth, and talent to the cause of the persecuted people, the Moravians.

These words of Christ from the cross say to us that no one, while he lives on earth, no matter how low he has sunk, is forsaken by God. While life remains, God is always waiting for the penitent one, ready to receive him back. Christ bore the grief and separation from God so that no other might again need to be forsaken or separated from the Father. We may and will suffer separation from the world and the enemies of Christ. We can expect loneliness and perhaps even mockery from Christ's enemies. But we need never again know separation from the support and salvation of God.

We learn from our Lord that, as we enter the dark experiences of life, when all hope or faith may seem at an end, the Scripture is our comfort and guide. Jesus, in the darkest hours of His life and of history itself, went to the Word of God for strength. He had previously hidden the Word in His heart and it came to His aid.

During World War II many persons went through what was called "brain washing." By the use of sophisticated and devilish devices those in control tried to wipe previous teachings from the minds of people so that they would function as commanded. It was reported that those who could stand the stress, and those who found inner strength to withstand the brain washing and torture, were those who had the Word of God hidden in their memories.

Jesus teaches us also, in these words from the cross, that in the difficult and dark hours we need to continue to trust God, the Father. Jesus trusted Him implicitly. God will not forsake us, even though we may feel forsaken. Jesus kept hold of God in the darkness even when He felt God had lost His hold on Him. So we need not receive an explanation for everything which happens. Rather we can be assured that in every experience we will ever face, the Father is there. The psalmist was so persuaded of God's presence that he cried, "Though I make my bed in hell, God is there."

Dr. Arthur Gossip's first sermon after his wife's sudden death was entitled, "When Life Tumbles In, What Then?" He answered it in his sermon. A part of what he said was: "I don't think you need to be afraid of life. Our hearts are very frail, and there are places where the road is very steep and very lonely. But we have a wonderful God. Who can separate us from His love? No, not death! For, standing in the roaring of Jordon, cold to the heart with its dreadful chill, and very conscious of the terror of its rushing, I too, like Hopeful, can call back to you who one day in your turn will have to cross it. 'Be of good cheer, my brother, for I feel the bottom and it is sound.' "

In the first half of the nineteenth century Charlotte Bronte, who died before forty years of age, wrote meaningful words: "Most people have had a period or periods in their lives when they have felt thus forsaken; when, having long hoped against hope, and still seen the day of fruition deferred, their hearts have truly sickened within them. This is a terrible hour, but it is often that darkest point which precedes the light of day; that turn of the year when the icy January wind carries over the waste at once the dirge of departing winter, and the prophecy of coming spring. The perishing birds, however, Christ understood the blast before which they shiver; and as little can the suffering soul recognize, in the climax of its affliction, the dawn of its deliverance. Yet, let whoever grieves still cling fast to love and faith in God; God will never deceive, never finally desert him. 'Whom He loveth, He chasteneth.' These words are true, and should not be forgotten."

What else do we learn from the suffering of our Lord? We learn that Jesus, in sounding the depth of human suffering and hope is One who is touched with "the feelings of our infirmities." The cross encompasses all human experiences. He has sounded the depth and no matter how far down we may go, we can know Jesus is there with us. He can help us because He has gone through it all.

Through all the depths of sin and loss
Sinks the plummet of His cross.
Never yet abyss was found
Deeper than that cross could sound.

There amid the ruins of sin, forever stands the cross, with God in the shadows supporting, standing by, able to save to the uttermost.

Finally, the great obstinate "Why?" of Jesus will still be with us as long as this world continues. We probably will never reach the place or stage where we shall cease asking, Why? One of the most incomprehensible mysteries is that God allows His chosen people to pass through spiritual darkness. As one has written, "All the millions of whys which have arisen from agonized souls, jealous for the honor of God, but perplexed by His providence, were concentrated in the why of Christ."

But the glorious fact remains that God has a way of bringing glory and good out of suffering. Dr. John H. Hutton of England said, "As a matter of history, life has rarely been accused or denounced by really great sufferers. Like our Lord, all the great sufferers, the martyr-spirits, have not cursed life, but blessed it.''

William Ralph Inge in *Speculum Animal* writes: ''The good news of Christianity is that suffering is itself divine. It is not foreign to the experience of God Himself. 'In all their affliction He was afflicted.' 'Surely He hath borne our grief and carried our sorrows.' 'If thou be the Son of God,' said His enemies, 'come down from the cross.' No! Not while any man remains unredeemed. It is the necessary form which divine love takes when it is brought into contact with evil. To overcome evil with good means to suffer unjustly and willingly.''

How often we learn our finest lessons from suffering! How often the things we seek so hard to avoid are those which, in the end, we cannot mature without! How many times the difficult and dark days of life helped us see the sunshine and blessings better than ever before!

Sir Walter Scott in *The Monastery* says some beautiful words which we know down deep are as true as they are difficult. ''There are those to whom a sense of religion has come in storm and tempest; there are those whom it has summoned amid scenes of revelry and idle vanity; there are those, too, who have heard its still small voice amid rural leisure and placid contentment. But perhaps the knowledge which causeth not to err, is most frequently impressed upon the mind during seasons of affliction: and tears are often the softened showers which cause the seed of heaven to spring and take root in the human heart.''

5

The Word of Companionship

I thirst.

† † †

† † † † †

At the inhumane prison in Germany every Friday the Nazis made the prisoners undress for medical inspection. They were humiliated. The women had to march before grinning guards. On one of those mornings Corrie ten Boom says, "Yet another page in the Bible leapt into life for me. 'He hung naked on the cross.' I had not known—had not thought . . . the paintings, the carved crucifixes showed at least a scrap of cloth. But this, I suddenly knew, was the respect and reverence of the artist. But oh—at the time itself, on that other Friday morning—there had been no reverence. No more than I saw in the faces around us now.

"I leaned toward Betsie, ahead of me in line. Her shoulder blades stood so sharp and thin beneath her blue and mottled skin. 'Betsie, they took *His* clothes too.'

"Ahead of me I heard a gasp. 'Oh, Corrie. And I never thanked Him . . .' " (p. 196, *The Hiding Place,* Fleming H. Revell Co.).

† † †

Christ walked where we now walk. In other religions of the world God is on a mountain or in a temple or in nirvana or sitting on a pedestal, far removed from human experience. In the Christian faith, however, we gladly sing,

> Jesus walked this lonesome valley,
> He had to walk it by Himself;
> Nobody else could walk it for Him,
> He had to walk it by Himself.

He was here. He knows what it is to be a human being. He knows what it is to be flesh and blood, bones and fingernails. He knows what it is to be criticized and betrayed. He knows temptation and grief. He knows physical suffering and emotional pain. And, always when we pray, let us remember that He understands because he was already here.

5

The Word of Companionship

After this, Jesus knowing that all things were now accomplished, that the scriptures might be fulfilled, saith, I thirst (John 19:28).

Ronald C. Wallace, in his fine book, *Words of Triumph,* illustrates the identification of Christ with us, as our companion in suffering, when He utters this word, "I thirst."

"When the people of Samaria, during a harrowing seige, had sunk so low in human barbarity as to eat their own children and fight over whose child should be next, a case of cannibalism was brought before the king for judgment. He had been among them all through the seige, but had appeared distant and aloof. But when this proof of the wretchedness of his people was brought to him, he cried and tore his clothes. The people suddenly saw that beneath all the splendor of his royal raiment, 'Behold, he had sackcloth within upon his flesh' (2 Kings 6:30). How closely the sight of that sackcloth must have bound Israel to their king. If they had misunderstood his disciplined calm as lack of concern, now they knew that he felt like them and for them, and his calmness had been the self-discipline of love for their sake.

"This cry 'I thirst,' like the king's sackcloth, brings to light again Jesus' constant and complete sharing of our human lot, reminding us that if it was hidden at times even during His days on earth, it was concealed only for the sake of those whose lot He so fully shared" (p. 63, John Knox Press, 1964).

Companionship in Humanity—Our Deliverance

Until now we saw Christ in His majesty. Previously He prayed the prayer of forgiveness for His persecutors. He admitted the repentant thief into the Kingdom. He demonstrated His care for His mother. Even in His forsakenness He moved in "solitary majesty." Now Christ from the cross reflects His complete and full humanity. Here we see again, in a real sense, the "word became flesh." As the Hebrew writer says later, "But we see Jesus, who was made a little lower than the angels for the suffering of death, crowned with glory and honour; that he by the grace of God should taste death for every man. For it became him, for whom are all things, and by whom are all things, in bringing many sons unto glory, to make the captain of their salvation perfect through sufferings. . . . Forasmuch then as the children are partakers of flesh and blood, he also himself likewise took part of the same; that through death he might destroy him that had the power of death, that is, the devil; And deliver them who through fear of death were all their lifetime subject to bondage. . . . Wherefore in all things it behoved him to be *made like unto his brethren*, that he might be a merciful and faithful high priest in things pertaining to God, to make reconciliation for the sins of the people. For in that he himself hath suffered being tempted, he is able to succour them that are tempted" (Heb. 2:9–18).

Possibly the last three statements from the cross were spoken in rapid succession. The end was near. This fifth statement, shortest and simplest of them all, reflects Christ's human physical suffering. The fourth word echoed the deep suffering of the soul. The fifth word speaks of the depth of physical suffering. In this word

He shows that He is our companion in physical suffering. He knows all our suffering. He knows the severest pain, the pangs of hunger, the longing for water. We now know that He has been through everything which can possibly come to us in life. And if He endured all we will ever endure, we know He is no longer far away. The Almighty and Holy One shares our suffering and assumes it completely.

And because He suffered He is able to save us, to assist us, and to lift us up, regardless of our situation. He is able to save us to the uttermost as we come unto God by Him.

John R. Mott wrote years ago: "Christ offers to men what other religions cannot. Let me illustrate by a man who cannot swim being cast into a lake. What is the best word Confucious has for the man who is sinking? 'Profit by your experience.' What is the most hopeful message which Buddah has for him? 'Struggle.' What is the most encouraging teaching of Hinduism for the sinking man? 'You may have another opportunity in the next incarnation.' What does Mohammed say? 'Whether you sink or whether you survive, it is the will of God.' And what does Jesus Christ say? 'Take my hand.' "

Many years ago a medical missionary in China was doing research on a certain disease for which there had been no apparent cure. His laboratory experiments were not satisfactory, and he was making no progress. Finally he realized that his difficulty was caused by the lack of proper facilities for studying the germ. He had no laboratory in China that could afford the equipment he needed.

What could he do? His furlough was approaching and he knew that he had to leave China shortly. Because he did not want to abandon his task, he considered taking a man who had the disease to the United States so that he could be placed in a hospital for observation and investigation. Such procedure however was impossible because of immigration laws. His experiments seemed doomed to failure.

At last he hit upon a solution to the problem. When his family was at church on Sunday morning just before leaving for furlough, he went into the laboratory, took a vial of the germs, poured them into a glass of fruit juice, and calmly swallowed it.

Because the disease did not take hold immediately he passed the immigration authorities. But he was not long in the United States until he recognized in himself the symptoms of the disease. He went to the hospital and made himself the subject of the necessary medical research, with the result that an antidote was found for the malady.

This doctor was not a savior in the sense that Christ was, for no other person can take away humanity's greatest malady—sin. However he was following in the footsteps of the Lord by entering into the problem and into the fellowship of the suffering ones. By doing so, he delivered them.

In the history of Moravian missions there is a similar story of sacrifice. We read of a missionary in the eighteenth century who felt called to make Jesus Christ known to the downtrodden, suffering slaves in the West Indies. So hard was their lot, so mercilessly were they treated, that they felt the bitterest distrust and hostility toward not only their masters but toward all white men. Because of this bitterness, the Moravian misssionary was unable to win a hearing for his message.

Daily this missionary prayed and pondered how to win the confidence of these slaves. How could he ever convince them of the meaning of the Gospel?

At last the answer came to him. He could reach them only by sharing their lot, even as Jesus shared the lot of humanity. Unhesitatingly the Moravian missionary relinquished his freedom, which was so precious that men died to preserve it. Because of his love for Christ and for those slaves, his brothers under God, the missionary sold himself into slavery. He sacrificed by sharing their food and privation. At last he won access to their hearts and a hearing for the Christ who died on the cross.

Companionship In Weakness—Our Strength

Jesus, as He had fulfilled all things written in the Old Testament concerning Himself, now, because He had immersed Himself in the Scriptures, knew that the prophesy of Psalm 69 must be fulfilled. How well the passage portrayed His present suffering!

"Reproach hath broken mine heart; and I am full of heaviness: and I looked for some to take pity, but there was none; and for comforters, but I found none. They gave me also gall for my meat; and in my thirst they gave me vinegar to drink" (Ps. 69:20–21).

In Jesus' cry, "I thirst," we hear the cry of supreme suffering. The pangs of thirst are the most terrible known by the human body. This cry climaxes the anguish of the cross. "And straightway one of them ran, and took a sponge, and filled it with vinegar, and put it on a reed, and gave him to drink" (Matt. 27:48). This is the second time it was offered to Christ. Hours before, He had refused the stupefying drug. He was determined to endure the agony of the cross with a clear mind. Now His suffering was at an end.

He who changed water into wine by His all-surpassing power; He who was the water of life; He who taught the beauty of giving water to those in need; He who offered water to the woman of Samaria; He who promised to those who believe living water flowing out from Himself; is now helplessly dependent upon His enemies. And even brutal men and the connivings of the wicked can be used by God to fulfill in detail His plan for salvation. Here, even when it seems wickedness is winning, we see God's initiative in triumph over the folly of men.

To be able to see God at work, and to trust that He is at work in our wicked world, gives strength to continue. This assurance turns our sobs to shouts, our sorrow to joy, our defeats to victory, and our unbelief to confident faith. God has the final word.

Yes, Christ had the power to quench His own thirst. His

greater power is demonstrated in His restraint from doing so. He became weak so that we might be made strong no matter what the anguish or suffering. Phillipians 2:6–8 tells us that He willingly divested Himself of His power and glory in order to be one with us in all our human needs. He was willing to hunger and thirst. He endured loneliness and pain. He was weary. He wept. He willingly did it all in human weakness.

Knowing that Jesus served God faithfully and perfectly in the form of human weakness forces us to lift up our heads when we become weak. If the hand of God was effective on Jesus, advancing the kingdom through extreme frailty, the same hand can be effective in whatever weakness we may endure. We find comfort in knowing that Christ advanced redemption through weakness. We also find comfort in knowing that God works out His purposes through those who continue to trust Him even in their hour of weakness.

Since Christ's death, the cross is a symbol of hope. How? Why? The gallows or guillotine or firing squad are never thought of as such a symbol. Yet the cross, considered the crudest instrument of death ever devised, is placed high on churches, altars, and hillsides as a symbol of hope, as a sign of God's love and compassion.

Prior to Christ's crucifixion the cross was a symbol of defeat, despair, and death. It spoke of shame, punishment, and weakness, for the one dying on a cross was exposed to every passerby. He was suffering severe judgment for his sin, and he was helpless to stop it.

In contrast, the cross now conveys the symbol of love, forgiveness, compassion, and power. For at the center of the centuries God placed a cross and on that cross He demonstrated the depth, the length, the width, and the breadth of His love for us. Through the cross is preached the forgiveness of sins because Christ died in our place and God says that if we, by faith, accept that fact, we are forgiven.

Through the cross "the Lord has comforted his people, and will have mercy on his afflicted" (Isa. 49:13).

> In the cross of Christ I glory,
> Tow'ring o'er the wrecks of time;
> All the light of sacred story,
> Gathers round its head sublime.

Companionship in Suffering—Our Cross

All Christian roads converge upon Calvary. The cross was Christ's crown. And He said we also, as His followers, will experience the cross. We are His followers, His disciples, as we take up the cross, which is the price of any sacrifice or suffering we bear for following Him. The cross is the cost a person pays in being His disciple.

One illuminated day the apostle Paul expressed the desire of his soul by saying, "That I may know him, and the power of his resurrection, and the fellowship of his sufferings" (Phil 3:10). For Paul it was more than a program. The cross was a passion. The life of suffering was more than an ideal. It was an experience. Hear the old crusader: "Of the Jews five times received I forty stripes save one. Thrice was I beaten with rods, once was I stoned, thrice I suffered shipwreck, a night and a day I have been in the deep: In journeyings often, in perils of waters, in perils of robbers, in perils by mine own countrymen, in perils by the heathen, in perils in the city, in perils in the wilderness, in perils in the sea, in perils among false brethren; in weariness and painfulness, in watchings often, in hunger and thirst, in fastings often, in cold and nakedness" (2 Cor. 11:24–27). He knew the fellowship of Christ's sufferings.

Sir Wilfred Grenfell, prophet of Labrador, who gave more than forty years of his heroic life as a medical missionary to that needy and neglected land of snow and ice, states: "The most orthodox faith is but a sounding brass unless it takes the form of personal sacrifice."

We do not understand the cross of Christ because we steer so clear of suffering. Says Edward Jeffries Rees, "It is not sufficient for modern Christians to go into joyful ecstasy in the anticipation of the power of the resurrection, and at the same moment go into blind forgetfulness over the necessity of a personal experience of the fellowship of Christ's suffering. Without the fellowship of the suffering, there is no power of the resurrection."

This is a day of flabby, fluctuating faith, when the heroism of the soul seems to have crawled into comfortable seclusion, and says W. E. Orchard, "It may take a crucified church to bring a crucified Christ before the eyes of the world."

In the seventeenth century in the town of Aigues-Mortes in Southern France, a beautiful and bright fourteen-year-old girl named Maria Durant was brought before the authorities. They demanded that she deny her Christian faith. Maria was not asked to commit any immoral act, to become a criminal, or even to change her day-by-day behavior. She was only asked to say, "J'abjure." No more, no less. She did not comply. Together with thirty other Huguenot women she was put into a tower by the sea.

It was not so much to say "J'abjure." It slides readily over the lips. It seems such a small price to pay for the sweetness of youth and the dignity of marriage, for a home full of children, a place by the village well, and the respect and love of neighbors. For thirty-eight years she continued to hold firm. She would not renounce her faith. And instead of the word of denial she, together with her fellow-martyrs, scratched in the prison wall the single word, "Resistez," resist!

This word is still seen on the stone wall at Aigues-Mortes. It is gaped at by tourists. For us today it is inexplicable. We do not understand the terrifying simplicity of a religious commitment which asks nothing of time and gets nothing from time. We cannot understand a faith which is not nourished by the temporal hope that tomorrow will be better.

To sit in a prison room thirty years and see the day change into night, and summer to autumn, to feel the slow systematic changes within one's flesh in the drying and wrinkling of the skin, in the loose muscle tone, to experience the stiffening of the joints and the slow stupefaction of the senses, to feel all this and still to persevere seems almost idiotic to this generation.

But to be a Christian is to be a partner in Christ's passion. It is to be a confessor, in the ancient sense, that is, to take a position regardless of the consequences. It is not to relinquish the first love, not to cool, not to betray.

An Indian mystic wrote, "The human heart cannot hold within itself two great loyalties." Jesus said: "You are for me or against me. You gather with me or else you scatter abroad. You cannot serve two masters." And to serve will mean a cross, a bearing of His suffering and His shame. He who bleeds also blesses. And said Francis Quarles:

> The way to bless lies not on beds of down,
> And he that has no cross deserves no crown.

Companionship in Death—Our Peace

In the evening of life the rays of the cross lengthen out through the dark valley of death, lighting the path for our feet. On either side may be the shadows of night, but in the sunlight rays we see the way to perfect day.

How often have we seen a peaceful follower of the cross as he passes from this life to the great beyond! In the consciousness of Christ's presence, in the knowledge of Christ's accomplishment on Calvary, there comes to the soul a wonderful peace, and to the heart a wondrous joy, even in death. Through His death He destroyed Satan, who brought death, leading mankind to sin. Through His death, Christ has delivered all who, through fear of death, lived in bondage.

Thus the death of the Christian is the finest witness to the power of Christ's cross. In the presence of such scenes all the words of skepticism and atheism are overthrown.

The invitation of the cross is given as long as life shall last. We must possess the promise of God here and now, through the pardon of the cross, before we can claim, in that final home, the companionship of Christ.

Father Peto and Elstowe dared to speak out bravely against Henry the Eighth's wrongs. They were summoned before the King's counsel to receive a reprimand. Lord Essex told them they deserved to be sewed into a sack and thrown into the Thames river. "Threaten such things to rich and dainty folk, who have their hope in this world," answered Elstowe, gallantly. "We fear them not; with thanks to God, we know the way to heaven to us reaching by water or by land." Men of such mettle might be broken or killed, but they could not be bent. They had settled their commitment to the Christ of Calvary and nothing could disturb their peace.

Finally we cannot but feel that Christ uttered these words, "I thirst," as a last appeal to those most responsible for His death. Certainly in His death He thirsted. It is said that those who die on a cross die either from thirst or suffocation. But isn't it striking that the only other time in the Gospels Jesus thirsted was with the woman at the well? There it was an invitation, a ground for contact. There is no record of His receiving a drink by the well of Samaria. But that woman did run back and tell the city about the Christ.

Certainly we would think those who knew the Scriptures so well would also see in Jesus' statement, "I thirst," with all which had preceded, the fulfillment of the Scripture. Was it one last appeal of the Savior for their salvation? But their foolish hearts were hardened.

Thank God, that until He comes again, we can drink at the satisfying fountain of Calvary because of Him who said, "If any man thirst, let him come unto me, and drink" (John 7:37). His final word to us is, "And the Spirit and the bride [church] say, Come . . . And let him that is athirst [lost person] come. And whosoever will, let him take the water of life freely" (Rev. 22:17).

I heard the voice of Jesus say:
  Behold I freely give
The living water—thirsty one,
  Stoop down, and drink and live!
I came to Jesus, and I drank
  Of that life-giving stream;
My thirst was quenched, my soul revived
  And now I live in Him.

6

The Word of Completion

It is finished.

† † †

† † † † †

"One word has made a life: one word has marred a life. One word has shaped the destinies of empires and altered the course of history. Mightiest of them this single word from the cross answers the hopes and fears of all the years: Finished! That shout rang back against the current of time to the beginning of man's transgression and provided the means of cancellation of transgression for every penitent soul. That shout ran forward to the end of the ages, declaring the fact of salvation accomplished for every believer. That shout ascended to the throne of God, and gladdened the heart of the Father and of the angels; that shout descended to the spirits of men in prison, and prepared them for the moment approaching when He should lead captivity captive, and give gifts unto men.

"Finished was all that prophecy had foretold.

In Him the shadows of the law
are all fulfilled, and now withdraw.

"Finished all that the Father had given Him to do. Our Fathers, the good and godly men of old, loved to dwell upon 'the finished work of the Redeemer.' He was able to say it of sin. The time had come to an end of which Daniel had foretold, 'to finish transgression, and to make an end of sins, and to make reconciliation for iniquity, and to bring in everlasting righteousness and to seal up vision and prophecy, and to anoint the most holy' " (pp. 110–111, *Testament of Love,* Hubert L. Simpson, Hodder & Stoughton, 1934).

6

The Word of Completion

"When Jesus had received the vinegar, he said, 'It is finished'; and he bowed his head and gave up his spirit'' (John 19:30, RSV).

While traveling by train a man sang softly to himself the song, "I Have Been Redeemed." Few people were on the train, but a man in the next seat joined him in singing. After the song the first singer turned to the stranger who had joined him and asked, "Have you been redeemed?" "Yes, praise God I have." "How long ago?" asked the first man. "A little more than nineteen hundred years ago," he replied, "but I'm sorry to say it was not much more than a year ago that I've known it and believed it."

Like the fifth phrase from the cross, this sixth statement is a single word. And it was no fluttering word of dying breath. It was a loud shout, so triumphant and unexpected that the curious crowd standing nearby was startled and fled back to Jerusalem. The centurion on duty sprang to attention, saying, "Truly this was the Son of God!"

Many call this word the greatest word in the history of human language, the single, most important verb Jesus ever spoke, the greatest proclamation ever given to mankind. It comprehends within it the salvation of the world. If the words, "My God, my God, why have you forsaken me?" are words of desolation, and the words, "I thirst," are words of lamentation, this word is a word of jubilation. Other words mark the deepest depth of Christ's humiliation. This word contains the consummation of His incarnation and His mission. Herein is wrapped the Gospel of God in Christ. Here is the finished work of Christ. Here is the ground of our assurance.

"It is finished" is not the word for giving up in the swoon of exhaustion. It is the note of triumph, the shout of conquest, the voice of victory. It is achievement. All He had come to do was complete.

At the time, it seemed like the last sigh of a suffering, despised, dying criminal. Those gathered, with a few exceptions, imagined only a mocked, forsaken, broken, bleeding, derided, deluded, and dying man. To them it sounded like the last cry of defeat and death. Who tried to understand or remember?

This word, "It is finished," is written in each of the first three Gospels. And each Gospel writer tells us the word was spoken with a loud voice. It was a shout of triumph, not of tragedy. It was a shout of jubilation, not lamentation. It was a cry of completeness and not of collapse. It was not "a whisper of agony" as one writer says, but a shout of victory, the cry of a conqueror.

Today we have derivatives from the same root of the verb in the original language in such words as telephone, telegraph, and television, which mean that a word, a message, a vision is carried to its intended destination and conclusion. It means the work is complete. In this sense, as the atmosphere of completeness covers Calvary, we ask: What is completed?

Suffering Is Consummated

Now the end of all Jesus' human suffering was come. The years of humiliation and heartbreak, the times of tension and trouble, treachery and tribulation, the misunderstanding and misdeeds against Him, were over. A long, drawn-out suffering marked all His days. And now His suffering in Gethsemane and on the cross came to the climax and crisis.

Yes, the endless hours of suffering were over. He had tried to prepare His disciples for this hour. They all shrank from it. Praying in the garden, Jesus confessed His own dread of so difficult a cup to drink. Now on the cross He drained it to its uttermost dregs and cried, "It is finished."

Beyond the intense physical suffering, Jesus knew, as no one has ever known, the agony over sin working in the world. Now He felt the bitterness of its consequences as if He Himself were the only one involved in all sin. He had wept and suffered at the sepulchre of Lazarus. Now He "tasted death for every man." The cup He begged God to spare Him was now taken and pressed to His lips.

Those who dogged His steps by malice and cunning could go no farther. The tempter who trailed Him, trying to turn Him from the Father's will, was forever defeated.

Satan is Conquered

How Satan sought to destroy Christ throughout His entire life! At Jesus' birth in Bethlehem, then in Nazareth and throughout His ministry, the devil tried to destroy Him physically. How subtly Satan tried to destroy Christ by temptations in the wilderness, through seducings by material things, miracles, and the might of power. Satan tried to destroy Christ in his efforts to turn Him aside through those closest to Him. In every way, Satan tried to turn Him from His mission.

Christ constantly carried the full load of the devil's attack. He faced every battle we face. Once He was on the cross, sin and evil made its final and fiercest assult. At the crucifixion, Satan forged his worst weapons. It is as if all nature did its worst against Him. Satan took the iron, mined by the hard hearts of sinful men, and made it into cruel nails to be driven into His hands and feet. He brought a beautiful spray of roses which through deceit and hypocrisy was stripped of all its colorful blossoms, and made into a cruel crown of thorns. The devil took a lovely tree—twisted it by hate, malice, and envy—and fashioned a bloody cross. Then when he had Christ helpless on the cross, he hurled, through those about, the awful words, "If you are the Son of God, come down and we will believe in you."

But because Christ stayed on the cross, we speak today of the victory of the cross. By dying He dislodged all Satan's snares and defeated forever the powers of the devil. In crying, "It is finished," our Lord tells us that He was conqueror. He invaded the very camp of the enemy by coming to earth and not yielding to temptation. And He emerged victorious.

Samuel Stennet put the words in poetry:

> 'Tis finished!' so the Savior cried.
> And meekly bowed His head and died;
> The battle fought, the victory won.

How often Christ referred to Himself as engaged in this fierce battle with Satan. When Jesus heard that things were going well in the mission of His disciples, He said, "I beheld Satan as lightning fall from heaven" (Luke 10:18). When the vested religious interests of His day opposed His mission, He described His enemies as being "of your father the devil." When He fought against what He called "the world," He described His conflict as against satanic power and said, "The prince of this world cometh, and hath nothing in me" (John 14:30). He described His death as both "mine hour" and also as the hour of His enemies and the "power of darkness." This was the decisive battle when all hell warred against God and His Christ.

The preaching of the apostles was in line with this conviction of the completeness of the sacrifice, achievements, atonement, and victory of Jesus. They said that the powers which before spoiled the life of humanity and the good of God's creation were broken at the cross. In His death He led captivity captive and "spoiled principalities and powers" making a "show of them openly, triumphing over them" (Col. 2:15). They saw in His perfect life of obedience and suffering that "by one offering" He had "perfected for ever them that are sanctified" (Heb. 10:14), so that no other offering need be made for reconciliation with God. The prince of the power of the air is a defeated foe. We who are in Christ fight not for a victory but from a victory. We are partakers of His power. We are sharers of His victory.

Paul, the apostle, in that great paragon in the second chapter of Colossians says, "You, who were spiritually dead because of your sins . . . God has now made to share in the very life of Christ! He has forgiven you all your sins; he has utterly wiped out the written evidence of broken commandments which always hung over our heads, and has completely annulled it by nailing it to the cross. And then, having drawn the sting of all the powers and authorities ranged against us, he exposed them, shattered, empty, and defeated, in his own triumphant victory!" (Col. 2:13–15, *Phillips*).

Thus is the victory of the cross—the dislodgement, doom, defeat of Satan and evil. This victory issues in the cry of victory for us, so that no longer do we need to be the dupes of the devil. We do not need to yield to sin. In Christ we are victorious.

Andrew W. Blackwood Jr., in his book, *The Voice of the Cross,* writes: "The forgiveness of sins is the backward look of redemption. The forward look of faith means victory over temptation. You can try a moral experiment, whether you be a Christian or not. When you are tempted to do something wrong, bring before your mind's eye the picture of our Savior's cross. Do not try to explain the cross, do not argue about it, just look at it. The temptation will lose its power. It has been the experience of thousands that the redemptive power of divine suffering love genuinely redeems" (p. 61, Baker).

Salvation Is Completed

Jesus' death on the cross was the completion of what Christ came to do. He gave His life for us all and cried, "It is finished." He is reporting now to the Father, "I have finished the work you gave me to do. My mission is accomplished. The reason I left glory and came to earth is realized. No stone in the structure of my messianic mission is missing."

Christ is also reporting to all mankind: all that can be done for our salvation is done. God's work of redemption is finished. The debt is paid. God and man are reconciled. God did His all for us through His Son on the cross. He can do no more. That's it! Now it is for us to respond. God moved on the cross and He can do no more until we make our move. We must move to accept what Christ did for us. He built the bridge to God. He paid the price of our redemption. He completed the work of salvation. Scripture says, "As many as received him, to them gave he the power to become the sons of God, even to those that believe on his name."

Years ago a picture was painted for the royal corps of Signallers in England. A signaller unarmed, lay dead in no-man's land. He had been sent out to repair a cable snapped by shell fire and so restore contact again. The picture showed him lying dead in the fulfillment of his task, holding together in his stiffened hands the broken ends, so the current could go through. Beneath the picture is one word, "Contact."

So Christ, through the cross, connects us again with God. Sin had snapped the connection. Christ brought the broken ends together in His death. Beneath the cross of Calvary we write one word, "Through." Through Him we are again brought back to God. It is through our Lord Jesus Christ that we are delivered from sin unto righteousness. Through Him we move from failure to victory. Through Jesus we move from death to life and from time to eternal bliss.

He was wounded for our transgressions,
He was bruised for our iniquities:
The chastisement of our peace was upon him;
And with His stripes we are healed (Isa. 53:5).

Jesus completed the task God gave Him to do. He laid down His life for us all and declared, "It is finished."

In his book on *The Seven Sayings of Christ on the Cross,* Dr. Anderson-Berry takes from history the striking antithesis to the meaning and glory of the finished work of Christ. Elizabeth, Queen of England, the idol of society and the leader in European fashion, when on her deathbed turned to her lady-in-waiting, and said, "O my God! It is over. I have come to the end of it—the end, the end. To have only one life, and to have done with it! To have lived, and loved, and triumphed; and now to know it is over! One may defy everything else but this."

And the listener sat watching. In a few moments more the face, whose slight smile had brought courtiers to their feet, turned into a mask of lifeless clay, and returned the anxious gaze of her servant with nothing more than a vacant stare. Such was the end of one whose meteoric course was the envy of the world. It could not be said that she had "finished" anything, for with her, all was "vanity and vexation of spirit." How different the end of the Savior! "I have glorified Thee on the earth; I have finished the work which Thou gavest me to do."

So Theodore K. Finck says, "Christ's word does not carry the idea that a whistle blows and a workman drops his tools in the middle of the job to leave for lunch. It means that the job is complete." It is Jesus saying, "I have finished the work I came to do." The servant of the Father, on the cross, saw the travail of His soul and was satisfied now. The grave, the resurrection, and the ascension are a matter of vindication. They are a testimony of triumph. The fact of our salvation is accomplished. These are a confirmation of the completeness of Christ's work of salvation.

Arthur W. Pink wrote: "God has furnished at least four proofs that Christ did finish the work which was given Him to do. First, in the rending of the veil, which showed that the way to God was now open. Second, in the raising of Christ from the dead, which evidenced that God had accepted His sacrifice. Third, the exaltation of Christ to His own right hand, which demonstrated the value of Christ's work and the Father's delight in His person. Fourth, the sending to earth of the Holy Spirit to apply the virtues and benefits of Christ's atoning death'' (p. 114, *The Seven Sayings of the Savior on the Cross,* Bible Truth Depot, 1947).

Through the cross we are redeemed, reconciled, and restored. And we can join the old-time chorus.

> Tis the promise of God full salvation to give
> Unto him who on Jesus His Son will believe.
> Hallelujah, 'tis done, I believe on the Son,
> I am saved by the blood of the crucified one.
>
> There's a part in that chorus for you and for me,
> And the theme of our praise forever will be,
> Hallelujah, 'tis done, I believe on the Son,
> I'm saved by the blood of the crucified one.

When a candle is finished it is burned out, destroyed, dissipated. But when a cathedral is finished it is completed and ready for service and use. So Christ's word announces, not that life was over, but that the salvation He came to bring was completed and ready for all who believe.

Conclusion

Schubert died at thirty-one years of age and left us a parable of his life and all human life in his ''Unfinished Symphony.''

People today still marvel at the genius of Michelangelo. His skills in architecture, painting, and sculpture are known the world around. His finished work such as his statues of Moses and David are well-known. What many do not know is that, because of his tempermental nature, he left most of his sculptures unfinished. In the new Sacristy of Michelanglo in Florence, Italy, you may visit an entire hall filled with the unfinished works of Michelangelo.

So many scholars and persons down through the centuries left important parts of their work unfinished. Books and works of art lay incomplete in study and studio. Most had planned to complete their works, but life ended.

Not so with Jesus! He finished the work He came to do. He is called the Author and Finisher of our faith. Nothing more is needed for our salvation.

Christ's earthly work is finished. Ours is not. As long as there is one soul without the Savior, our work must go on. Christ did all that divine love could do to redeem the world. He left us the task of sharing that love in all of life.

Finally, will we accept the finished work of Christ and claim all the blessings He brings? Herein is the challenge and goal.

An elderly mountain lady in a shack on the side of a steep hill was approaching starvation. She received regular letters from a son who had promised her support when he left home, but the money did not arrive.

In her desperation she discussed her condition with her neighbor, who asked about her son. "He sends me letters," she said, "and always encloses pretty little pictures, but I never get money."

"Might I see the pictures your son sends?" asked the neighbor after some time. The poverty-stricken woman took him to her bedroom and showed him rows of "pictures" tacked on the wall—money orders worth thousands of dollars. She had received support, but through ignorance did not claim the blessings.

In the autobiography of Hudson Taylor, founder of the China Inland Mission, we find his testimony of how he became a follower of Jesus. At home alone one day, he looked for a book to read when time hung heavily on his hands. No book attracted him, so he turned over a basket of pamphlets and selected from among them a tract which looked interesting. "I knew," he said, "that it would have a story at the commencement and a moral at the close; but I promised myself that I would enjoy the story and leave the rest. It would be easy to put away the tract as soon as it should seem prosy."

Taylor tells that as he read he was struck by the expression, " 'The finished work of Christ.' Why, I asked myself, does the author use these terms? . . . Then the words 'It is finished' presented themselves to my mind. What is it that is finished? I asked, and in an instant my mind replied: A perfect expiation for sin; entire satisfaction has been given; the debt has been paid by the substitute."

Hudson Taylor saw in a new way that Christ died for the sins of all persons. He said to himself, "If, then, the entire work is finished, all the debt paid, what remains for me to do? In another instant the light was shed through my mind by the Holy Ghost, and the joyous conviction was given me that nothing more was to be done, save to fall on my knees, to accept this Savior and His love, to praise God forever."

7

The Word of Commitment

Father, into thy hands I commit my spirit.

† † †

† † † † †

Hershel H. Hobbs wrote: "It was my privilege to sit in the last class taught by A. T. Robertson. During the period this man, who had written a host of volumes interpreting the Greek New Testament, wrote four Greek words on the blackboard: polis, huper, onoma, and dimnaious. After his death shortly thereafter an enterprising student made pictures of these words. So cherished were they that he found a ready sale for the pictures among the students.

"If we cherish these last words written by a devoted follower of Jesus, how much more should we do so regarding the last words spoken by his Lord upon the cross. The words of the teacher have long since been crossed from the blackboard, but these words of the Savior are stamped indelibly in the very fabric of the universe in the hearts of the faithful. Had Dr. Robertson known that he was writing his last words, we wonder whether he might have chosen others, and what they would have been. Jesus knew that these were His final words before death. Furthermore, He was conscious of the fact that they would be read and studied through the ages. Therefore we may be certain that He who never spoke an idle word chose these words with deliberate care. That they are cherished by His followers is seen by those who in every age have chosen to die with them upon their lips" (p. 89, *The Crucial Words From Calvary,* Baker, 1958).

7

The Word of Commitment

Then Jesus, crying with a loud voice, said, "Father, into thy hands I commit my spirit!" (Luke 23:46, RSV*).*

Carroll S. Ringgold writes of a white cross which stood on the outskirts of a city. A young boy was lost in the city. A policeman asked, "Where do you live? Just tell me where you live." But the boy did not know his address. Finally, upon further questioning, the small boy said, "Take me to the cross on the hillside, and I can find my way home from there."

So God has placed a cross at the center of the centuries. And as we find the cross we find our way home again, here and hereafter. The cross is the bulletin board on which God nailed His message of redemption.

As we come to the final phrase from Christ on the cross, the conflict of the cross is past. The storm of suffering is at an end. As He had often done in His life, Christ now, in the last utterance before death, touched the deepest chords of the human heart and arrested the attention of the world. How much we want to know what God is like! How we need to commit ourselves to Him who is all-knowing and all-loving! And what can we say in the hour of death? These words possess more than beauty; they possess power. They possess more than wonder; they possess hope. They possess more than tribute; they possess triumph.

Dr. Henry Beets writes, "In olden days, when a victorious general was about to leave the field of battle, he would utter a loud cry as a token that he had triumphed. And so the great Captain of our salvation, as He was about to quit the battlefield of all His suffering, uttered a loud cry, as a token that He was victorious." "Father, into thy hands I commit my spirit."

Thus the Calvary curtain rises for the final scene, a scene only Luke shares with us. And how happy we are for this last word from our Lord. It is taken from Psalm 31:5 and without a doubt was the first prayer His mother Mary taught Him. Every Jewish child was taught this evening prayer. And now that very prayer is prayed by the Savior in the evening, the last moment, of His life.

In an old book called *The Testament of Love,* Hubert L. Simpson of England speaks of his ministering to a boy in his last moments of life. Doctors said the boy was beyond human help and hearing. So Simpson prayed out loud with the words the boy might have learned long before.

> This night I lay me down to sleep.
> I pray Thee, Lord, my soul to keep.
> And if I die before I wake—

Before he could finish the prayer, the young boy's eyes opened a moment, and there was radiance not of earth on his face, as taking the words, he finished triumphantly, "I pray Thee, Lord, my soul to take." "And so," says Simpson, "he went from this life with the words he had learned long before in a Highland home at his mother's knee." After some time Simpson went to the boy's mother and in response to her earnest question, "Are you sure my laddie's safe?" he told her of her son's last words.

So, as the sun set on His suffering, Jesus prayed the evening prayer of His boyhood, then breathed His last.

These last words of Christ were prayed in the final moment of life by a multitude of the faithful followers of Christ down through the centuries. Included in the long list are persons like Thomas A. Becket, martyred in 1170, and John Huss burned at the stake in 1415. The record says that as the flames of fire choked Huss, he with a merry and cheerful countenance said, "Into Thy hands I commend my spirit." So also Polycarp, Bernard, Jerome of Prague, and John Knox. Martin Luther said in his last moments, "Blessed are they who die not only for the Lord as martyrs; not only in the Lord, as believers, but likewise with the Lord, as breathing forth their lives in the words, 'Father, into Thy hands I commend my spirit.' "

So these words for Christ and for His followers are not only the dying words of one who is leaving this life. These words are the final confession of faith of the one and the many who thought of themselves as in the hands of God, when things went well, and when suffering, sorrow, and death fell upon them. Such people surrender themselves, not into the hands of death or fate, but into the hands of a kind, heavenly Father.

The Receiving Father

Jesus added one word to the words from Psalm 31. He added the word, "Father." The first words from the cross and these last words from the cross begin with the same word. In prayer for His enemies Christ prayed, "Father, forgive them; for they know not what they do." Now, in the last breath of life He calls on the Father. In a real sense the word "Father" becomes *the* word of the cross. Here is the great revelation of Calvary.

And calling upon God as "Father" was not new to Jesus. The first recorded utterance of Jesus when, at twelve years of age, his family found Him in the temple was, "Don't you know I must be about my Father's business?" In the Sermon on the Mount, which may well be His first formal discourse recorded, He calls God "Father" seventeen times. And in His final discussion with

His disciples in John 14 through 16, Jesus speaks of God as "Father" forty-five times. In John 17 He calls God "Father" six times. It was Jesus who taught us to call upon God as Father in prayer. The word "Father" encompasses His whole concept of God throughout His life. And He invites us to speak to God, the Creator, the Sustainer and Savior, in terms of closest affection.

This is the revelation Christ gave us of God. It sums up His disclosure of God for us. God is a Father, a loving, compassionate Father in whom we can trust. The Father's hands—that was to Jesus the synonym for safety, strength, and security—upheld in life shall uphold hereafter.

Again and again down through the decades of time persons have asked the question, "How could God be Father and permit such cruel murder of His Son?" Or, "How could a Father stand by?" If we see only in the cross man's hate and injustice and prejudice, if we look at the cross merely as a martyr's death, then the word "Father" is the greatest mystery of the cross. It says God is guilty for not delivering His Son from evil men.

But if we believe the Scripture, which says that we are brought nigh by the blood of Christ, that through His death we are redeemed—restored again with God—that by His death He slew the enmity between us and God, we see that the Divine permission is an absolute necessity. Yes, it's true, perhaps the greatest temptation hurled at Him while on the cross was, "If you are the Son of God, come down." Certainly it was true as Christ told Pilate: "You could have no power against me except it were given you from above." Yet if He had come down, there would be no atonement. General William Booth spoke truth, "If Jesus had come down they might have believed on Him for a while. But the centuries have believed in Him because He stayed up."

God could show His displeasure and power now only in the darkness, the lightning and thunder, the rent veil, and the opening of the graves, that men might notice. But if salvation was to be finished, He could not deliver His own Son from death.

Yet how much it must have cost the Father! Putting the word "Father" into the fabric of the cross reveals the price of redemption. "Where was God when my son died?" a disheartened and disturbed father asked his pastor. "At the same place He was when His own son died," replied the minister. He was there, saddened, but allowing a greater purpose to be realized.

Now the darkness of forsakenness is past. The comfort of the Father's presence in love and protection is renewed. And faith returns in the joy of full assurance. How good to know that back of all the tangled skeins of human life is a loving Father. And, if God is our Father, is there anything that will separate us from His great love?

The enemies may be encamped all around, but in the light of Calvary and the Savior's cry, God is described as Father. Our enemies fold their tents and disappear with the breaking of the day. Who shall separate us from the love of such a Father? Paul's testimony remains for all saints to take up the strain, "I am persuaded, that neither death, nor life, nor angels, nor principalities, nor powers, nor things present, nor things to come, nor height, nor depth, nor any other creature, shall be able to separate us from the love of God, which is in Christ Jesus our Lord."

The Committing Son

Jesus, in His last conscious act, committed Himself to the Father. But it was consistant with His whole life. Commitment was not something done only at the end of life. It was daily. From childhood and throughout His ministry He constantly committed Himself to the work and will of God for Him.

In the teen times of life Jesus must be about His Father's business. In the middle years of His ministry He must do the work of Him who sent Him. In the temptation in the wilderness His food was to do the Father's will. In the last night in Gethsemane, the long night of agony and struggle is ended by "Abba, Father, nevertheless, not my will but Thine be done."

And when we believe in the Father we will commit ourselves in love and obedience to Him, and then relax in His care. Faith is committing ourselves completely into the Father's hand. Fear flows from a lack of commitment, or a lack of understanding, of the kind of Father we have. To commit is to trust in a God who has His hold on us, and it does not depend on our hold on Him. Then commitment results in peace, gratitude, and praise. All even death can do is to deliver us to our Father, where we shall be like Him, for we shall see Him as He is.

This word of Scripture Jesus used means more than a mere asking or hoping. It means an entrusting, a delivery over of oneself completely. It speaks of an attitude of trust which submits and entrusts ourselves, with all our fears and needs, knowing we can trust Him at all times for the outcome.

John W. Kennedy in *Advance In Light,* 1948, says, " 'Into Thy hands.' This final word of Jesus brings completion of faith for others, completion of faith for us. Faith in Him leads us at last to trust. We yield over all to Him because we believe what He said about God and life is true." Thus Paul could write Timothy, "I know whom I have believed, and am persuaded that he is able to keep that which I have commited unto him against that day" (2 Tim. 1:12).

"Trust in God," said Faber, "is the last of all things, and the whole of all things."

As a pastor I was called to minister to persons who were on their deathbeds. Particularly, because of the youthfulness of several, serious questions were raised regarding God's will and God's ability to heal. One mother struggled long with the meaning of faith. I shared with her that the greatest thing any of us can do is to completely trust God with our own lives and the lives of our families, even as Jesus trusted God and committed Himself to the Father. After this commitment, all is possible. Then we are prepared for healing to physical life or to receive the complete healing by entering heaven itself.

One thing more about the committal of Jesus. The Scripture says that Christ in a unique way commended His spirit to God. He willed to be born and to die. We have no choice. Not so with Christ. Men could not take Him until His hour was come.

Time and again people tried to make Him king or to kill Him. And each time He escaped their plan. Now in the last day of His life He gave Himself over to wicked men and in this, the last hour, committed Himself to the Father, never again to be at the mercies of the wicked. The ancient fathers delighted to dwell on this blessed contrast. He said of Himself, "I have power to lay it [my life] down, and I have power to take it again. This commandment have I received of my Father" (John 10:18).

The Departing Spirit

To Jesus, death was not a leap in the dark, a plunge into the unknown void, a walk in the cold stream of death, or a dark hour. These describe pagan ideas of death. To Jesus, death was a reunion with the Father. He committed Himself into the loving care of God. To Him death was an entrance into the Father's home. It is as if Jesus cried with a loud voice to command the portals of heaven to open and let Him enter into the presence of the Father.

Jesus commended His spirit unto God. The body does not possess the spirit so much as the spirit possess the body. The real person who feels, thinks, and wills is the spirit which suffers no decay. The real person passes through the portals of death into the regions beyond. This is the doctrine of immortality. And Christ's words from the cross declare it. If we do not live throughout eternity, more than half the Bible can be destroyed as worthless. And those who are Christ's move at death into the hands of God the Father. Scripture says, "To be absent from the body is to be present with the Lord." "If the earthly house of this tabernacle be destroyed, we have a building of God, not made with hands, eternal in the heavens."

Jesus changed the false concept, which made people deck

themselves in dark clothes of mourning at death, and tells us that death is the completion of giving ourselves over to the father. Paul, the apostle says, ‘‘If we live, we live unto him and if we die, we die unto him for whether we live or die, we are his.’’ Leaving this life, we pass into the hands of God.

F. B. Meyer, in his eighties, sat down to write a letter to a friend. ‘‘I have just heard to my surprise,’’ he said, ‘‘that I have only a few days to live. It may be before this reaches you, I shall have entered the palace. Don't trouble yourself to write. We shall meet in the morning. With much love. Yours affectionately.’’

That is triumph. That is no counterfeit comfort. That is reunion with the Father.

John Thornton received word he had only a few days to live. He tells how he sat at his window and looked out at the river before him and the mountains beyond. He looked at the stars shining in the sky. Then he wrote: ‘‘I'm going to leave. But river, I'll be alive when every drop in you has dried up. Mountains, I'll be alive when you have disappeared. Stars, I'll be around when your light has burned out. For my spirit goes to God who gave it. I commit myself into the hands of the Father.’’

The little maid, of whom Wordsworth wrote, wisely insisted that her departed brother and sister, taken by death, must also be counted as part of her family.

> 'How many are you, then' said I,
> 'If thy two are in heaven?'
> The little maiden did reply,
> 'Oh, Master, we are seven!'
> 'But they are dead—those two are dead,
> Their spirits are in heaven!'
> T'was throwing words away, but still
> The little maid would have her will,
> And said, 'Nay, we are seven!'

In this last prayer of His earthly life, our Lord taught us how to die. And in all generations the shout of the departing Savior rings out as a challenge before the everlasting doors of heaven. He spoke with a loud voice as if to say, "Let these words ring through the corridors of time and let them bring to all their message of assurance and peace."

With the small boy we say, "Take us to the cross on the hill. We can find our way home from there!"